Tongue in the Wind:
Chewy's Pawtobiography

In Christ,
Chewy's Driver
(Butd Ericq)

To Kathleen
from LSO L. Crowder
2019

Tongue in the Wind:
Chewy's Pawtobiography

As barktated by Chewy to his driver, Butch Ewing

With input from Chewy's mom, Jo Ewing

Unedited Version

Butch Ewing
2018

First Printing: 2018

ISBN: 978-1790652136

Butch Ewing
P.O. Box 46
Kipling, North Carolina 27543

www.bikerdoggie.com

Dedication

To God, to His Son, and to my lovely wife, Jo Ewing.

Thank you. Without the blessings of God, Jesus, and my wife, Chewy and I would not have been able to honor Fallen Heroes, passing veterans, military members (past and present), and their families, as well as support a number of non-profit organizations. Missions and events are where many of Chewy's stories and adventures originate.

Contents

Acknowledgements

I would like to thank my wife and our family and friends, with whose encouragement this book about Chewy's adventures became a reality.

Thank you to friends who consistently took pictures of Chewy at missions and events and posted them on social media. Each of them, and many more, helped to document events in Chewy's life: Bill "OB Jammer" Amerson, Charles Bullock, Dee "One More" James, Thomas "G.E." Sanders, Paula Schronce, Jo "Cuffey" Warren, Kathy "Whips" Whipkey, Mike "Krzywuf" Wilson, Ray Price Harley-Davidson (now, Tobacco Road Harley-Davidson), and many, many more.

Thank you to non-profit organizations who allowed Chewy to be affiliated with them: Freedom Biker Church, American Gold Star Mothers Dogwood and Magnolia Chapters, USO-NC, Patriot Rovers, and many more.

Thank you to organizations who allowed Chewy to remain a lone wolf and participate in events without holding formal memberships: Freedom Biker Church, Combat Veterans Motorcycle Association NC 15-1 & NC 15-6, Rolling Thunder NC1, NC4 & NC7, Raleigh H.O.G., Patriot Guard, No Rules Riders, and many more.

A special thank you to Debbie "Doobie" Sykes, the Editor-in-Chief of Behind Barz Motorcycle Magazine. Thank you for taking the risk and publishing Chewy's articles, as barktated by him.

Thank you to Thomas Sanders, who rode with Chewy across the USA in 2011. Together, we learned about travelling long distance with a dog on a motorcycle – and the delays we encountered as Chewy met new friends at each fuel stop, rest area, hotel, and eatery.

Thank you to Craig Hardy, who rode with Chewy in his 2014 attempt across the USA until our motorcycle broke down in West Virginia. We realized that success can be measured in more ways than reaching our planned destination – God had other plans for each of us.

Introduction

Chewy was a real dog who rode about 102,000 miles on a Harley-Davidson Ultra Classic. This book is written mostly from Chewy's perspective, as "barktated" to me (his driver and dad). The stories of his adventures are true.

Chewy "barktated" articles for Behind Barz Motorcycle Magazine from 2011 to 2015. The articles, like his social media page and most of this book, were written from Chewy's perspective. Those articles became the basis for this collection of short stories. This book contains details that could not be included in all of the Behind Barz articles.

Originally, this book was Chewy's "pawtobiography" and was started around 2011. When Chewy collapsed in 2015, we stopped working on his draft manuscript. When Chewy passed in 2017, I was unsure about completing his manuscript. About two and a half months after he passed, a Celebration of Life event was held at Freedom Biker Church in Clayton, North Carolina. Friends, Paula and Frank Schronce, videoed the Celebration. I listened to the audience's reactions when I told of how God used Chewy to reach people and told them about a few of Chewy's adventures, some being comical. Afterwards, countless people told me that the stories should be in a movie or that I should write a book. Most people didn't realize that the stories I told were already captured in this partially completed manuscript.

I adopted Chewy from a kill shelter in North Carolina on the day he was to be euthanized. Chewy was picked up as a stray. It was his third day at the SPCA. He feared people and showed signs of abuse. I battle PTSD demons and, perhaps, Chewy had a form of doggie PTSD. Perhaps he was neglected and/or mistreated. We bonded and, over the years together, we helped each other.

Chewy began riding a Harley-Davidson when he was about six years old. He took instantly to riding. Soon after his first ride, Steve Metz, who was the Director of the Raleigh Harley Owners Group (H.O.G.) at the time, speculated that Chewy could become one of the most photographed dogs in North Carolina. While on the road, countless people in cars, vans, pick-ups, 18-wheelers, etc. would smile and take pictures of Chewy. Fuel and rest stops that typically take 5-15 minutes could take an hour or more as people met Chewy, pet him, took photos of him and with him, and asked questions. God gave us a wonderful ministry opportunity to give people a glimpse into a life of a Christian – we're not perfect, but our faith is in a perfect God and a perfect Son.

Chewy in western North Carolina, returning from a trip to South Texas

Chewy earned a number of honorary titles and recognitions, which include:

- Associate Member, American Gold Star Mothers, Dogwood Chapter
- Ambassadog, USO of North Carolina
- Ambassadog, Carolina Patriot Rovers
- Repawter, Behind Barz Motorcycle Magazine
- Honorary Mascot, Combat Veterans Motorcycle Association Auxiliary, NC 15-1
- Honorary Mascot, MeanStreet Riders
- Selected as one of twenty North Carolina Local Heroes by the New York Says Thank You Foundation
- Received the Armed Forces Salute from WTVD (Raleigh, North Carolina's ABC television affiliate)

- United States flag flown in Chewy's honor on Veterans Day 2011 by Combined Forces Special Operations Component Command - Afghanistan
- United States flag flown at the North Carolina State Capitol and presented by a Gold Star Mother
- Featured in the first episode of a 10-episode TV series about USO of North Carolina (USO-NC)
- Featured in WRAL Tar Heel Traveler multiple times (WRAL is Raleigh, North Carolina's NBC television affiliate)
- "100 MPH Club", Charlotte Motor Speedway

Chewy presented with a US flag flown in Afghanistan on Veterans Day 2011 in his honor

Chewy completed two rides across the USA. In both rides, he couriered a Gold Star roster with thousands of names of service members who gave the ultimate sacrifice while in service to our country after the Vietnam War. In both rides, the west coast destination was the Northwood Gratitude and Honor Memorial in

Irvine, California. On his third cross country ride, our motorcycle broke down about 20 miles west of Summerville, West Virginia. Although we did not reach our destination in Irvine, California, that ride was successful in other ways.

Chewy completed three Iron Butt Saddle Sore 1000 events, riding 1000 miles in 24 hours with the Combat Veterans Motorcycle Association NC 15-1. CVMA gave him the road name "Iron Mutt". The CVMA Iron Butt events were known as Charlie Mikes, the military phonetic spelling of the letters CM, which is the acronym for "Continue the Mission". Each Charlie Mike was certified by the Iron Butt Association. Charlie Mike I honored the Vietnam War Veterans. Charlie Mike II honored the Korean War Veterans. Charlie Mike III honored the World War II Veterans.

Chewy collapsed on June 26 at the age of 12 or 13 in human years. Jo and I rushed Chewy to an emergency veterinarian. He was not expected to survive the night. The doctor suspected pheochromocytoma and made arrangements to transfer Chewy to the North Carolina State University Veterinary Hospital, where he was placed in doggie ICU. Within 12 hours of collapsing, thousands of people around the world prayed for Chewy after reading about his collapse in social media. God answered those prayers. On Chewy's third day in the hospital, he was released. He was expected to live only two to four weeks. People continued praying. Chewy had an excellent medical team with Dr Gene Bailey and Dr Lindsay Warner at Animal Hospital of Peak Plaza in Apex, North Carolina. God answered the countless prayers. Chewy lived another 22 months! Overall, he was pain free, but he tired easily and seemed to have occasional, short moments of discomfort. He would pass gas (sometimes loudly) and appear to feel better.

Two days before Chewy passed away, he was with the Patriot Guard in Lillington, North Carolina to honor a passing World War II veteran. The day before he passed, he attended a charity event in Fayetteville, North Carolina: Zuma 'round Town with Doctah Steve. Although he moved slowly, he appeared very happy and content to be attending events and being among bikers.

Chewy collapsed again on April 3. He was about 15. Jo and I could see that Chewy was not feeling well. The clinical signs indicated he was struggling. Jo and I made the difficult decision to help his earthly body go to eternal sleep. As Chewy drifted, Jo was sitting in front of him and I was lying next to him. Dr Warner and Tracy Vester talked us through the procedure. Chewy went very peacefully.

I never heard of a funeral for a dog and there were people inquiring about a Memorial Service for Chewy. Floyd Baker, a pastor at Freedom Biker Church in Clayton, North Carolina, and I discussed a service. Floyd suggested a Celebration of Life. He discussed the proposed event with Preacher Mike Beasley. On June 24, we celebrated Chewy's life with stories about how God used Chewy to reach people. The Celebration wasn't completely about Chewy – it was mostly about the ministry that God blessed upon Chewy. The adventures I told at Chewy's Celebration are in this book.

Due to God's influence on Jo, Chewy, and me, Chewy's pawtobiography begins the first chapter and ends the last chapter with God.

"Charlie Mike"
"Not Forgotten"

Butch Ewing
(Chewy's Driver)

Chapter 1: Finding my Furever Pawrents

GOD had a plan for me. He created all things. He has a purpose for everything He creates – even a furry guy like me and my broken hooman driver. In hindsight, we saw that placing the two of us together was part of His plan. Neither one of us had any idea that we would be biker brothers serving God.

It was early spring. I found myself in a cage with a concrete floor. I was lonely and afraid. It was my third day in the shelter and I was scheduled to have my life ended that morning. They called it overcrowding. I was being killed because I was born.

The front office received a call early in the morning. Someone is coming to see me. He will be here in about three hours. I gained a few hours of life. All I had was time.

The man arrived. A SPCA staff member put the man in a fenced, concrete-floored, large kennel area to wait for me. I was led into the area. I saw him. He didn't look familiar. He was in the center of the area. I was afraid. I leaned against the fence near the gate. I was trembling. He called for me in a gentle voice. "Come here, boy. Come here, buddy."

The staff member told the man that I was afraid of people and that I showed signs of being physically abused. The man dropped to his knees and called to me again. After several minutes, I gathered the courage to slowly walk towards him. I was trembling and I kept my head down. When I reached him, he gently petted me and talked to me. I wasn't sure what he was going to do with me. He gently rubbed my ribs and around my neck. The staff member told him that I had never gone to anyone like that. I was trembling, but it felt good having someone touch me and talk to me in a calm tone.

The man asked the staff member if he could spend time with me. The staff member agreed and departed. He talked to me and asked me questions.

"What's your name, buddy?"

"Where did you come from?"

"Why are you shaking?"

Even if I could speak hooman, I'm not sure I would have talked. I was very afraid of hoomans.

He stood up and stepped back from me. I stood up and faced him, not knowing what he was going to do to me. I thought maybe he was going to hit me or kick me. He said some words I didn't understand, like "sit". It sounded like he wanted me to do something, but I didn't know what he wanted. I wish I knew what those words meant. All I knew to do was tremble and lower my head. The man kneeled on the concrete floor again, and I leaned against him. He kept talking to me in a gentle voice. I gradually stopped trembling and became comfortable listening to him talk. I could sense that he was also feeling calmer as he petted me and talked to me. I think he needed a friend as much as I needed a friend.

When the staff member returned, the man asked how I came to this place. She said that I was found as a stray. It's possible that a military family moved, abandoned me, left me chained somewhere, and I eventually got free. The man seemed to be thinking while he looked at me. He asked the staff member if he could talk it over with his wife and get back to them tomorrow morning. The staff member replied that they were out of space. If I wasn't adopted, I would be put to sleep. The man looked at me in the eyes and said "Sorry, guy. I can't adopt you unless I can talk it over with my wife."

He stood up and walked towards the door.

"Wait! Where're you going?"

I hurried to follow him and got tangled in his legs, almost tripping him. He stopped, knelt down, and said "Sorry, buddy. I need to talk it over with my wife."

I snuggled up against him while he knelt and I leaned my weight into him. I gently licked his cheek and chin. He wrapped his arms around me, and I put my muzzle against his cheek. I didn't want him to go. We stayed in that position for a few seconds and I could sense that simple hug was making him feel different. He looked into my eyes for a few seconds, but it seemed like minutes. I could see his eyes starting to get watery. Then he said it quietly to me: "I don't know what Jo is going to say, but you're coming home." My ears perked up. "Home?" That sounds like a nice word!

The man told the SPCA staffer "I'm taking him home with me." I didn't understand what he said, but it sounded good and my ears perked up again. He said that word "home" again! She smiled.

My fellow doggie inmates barked from their kennels as I walked to the front of the building next to the man. The man was given papers to complete and sign. While he stood and wrote at the counter, I sat next to his feet and leaned against his leg. I wasn't letting this hooman go without me.

The manager asked for the name and phone number of a veterinarian. The man gave her the phone number of my future doctor, Dr Gene Bailey. The manager called the vet's office. After a few short minutes, she came around the counter. She told me that my new vet said I was going to a really good home and that I couldn't have a better daddy. I liked her voice tone when she said that. I was rescued from doggie death row!

One of the documents that my driver had to sign was an agreement to have me "fixed". The SPCA would reimburse my doctor a portion of the fees to have me "fixed". Fixed? I just needed to be loved. I didn't know I needed fixin'.

The manager put a blue color around my neck, and my dad led me outside to his car. My dad came prepared. He had a large doggie travel crate in the trunk that he quickly assembled in the parking lot. He placed the crate in the back seat of the big car. He led me into the crate. I was hesitant, so he gave me a boost and I willingly went into the crate and sat.

It was about a two-hour ride to my new home. As my dad drove and talked to me, I quietly looked around. I could see the back of my dad's head. Listening to my dad's voice was calming, and I wasn't trembling anymore. The windows of the car frequently went down, and I heard my dad laugh about the smell. Was that him or me? Yup, it was me! I had a terrible case of gas. It was smelly, but I couldn't do anything about it. My dad said my new mom would probably tell me that "there's more room out than there is in." He said she'll probably leave the room because there was fresher air out of that room than there was inside of that room.

We arrived at my new home. My dad opened the car door and the crate door, put a leash on me, and led me through the garage and into the house. I sniffed around inside the house. Interesting smells. I lifted my leg on a dining room chair to start marking and I heard my dad yell "No!" I squeezed it off, but leaked a little. My dad grabbed some paper towels. He made me watch him clean it up and he said that "No" word a lot while pointing to where I leaked. I lowered my head and put my ears back. I peed where I sat. I didn't like the way he said that word. I quickly understood "No!" meant I did something I wasn't supposed to do. I was trembling, but he didn't hit me. He took me outside on the leash. I sniffed around and marked some areas and my driver said "Good boy!" in a cheerful and excited tone. He petted me with excitement. I liked that! I learned quickly that I'm not supposed to mark inside the house. My driver told me many times that I'm smart and a quick learner.

After exploring the backyard for a few minutes, we returned inside the house. We walked by the chair that I tried to mark. I kept my distance from that chair. I sniffed a large aquarium that had huge, orange fishies – I had never seen fish or an aquarium. I sat on the floor next to my dad and watched the fish move to the left and move to the right for a few minutes.

My dad led me to a bedroom door and opened it. There was a teenage boy in there: Keith. Keith saw me and said "Wow!" He petted me while I sniffed him. Keith is my mom and dad's youngest son. Their oldest son, Matt, was married and lived several miles away.

My dad led me outside again. He and Keith gave me a bath. I don't like being wet, but I enjoyed them rubbing my fur. After drying me with a blow dryer, we went into the house. He laid a dry towel on the floor of the sun room. My dad and Keith spent the next hour pulling over 60 ticks from me. I was feeling relaxed laying on the floor with two sets of hands rubbing through my fur. They talked about my name. Smokey? Bear? Until they decided on my name, I had a few names, such as "Good Boy," "Duuuuuude," "No-no," and "Come here, boy." I learned that if I didn't stop at "no-no", that I would soon hear a louder and sterner "NO!" Hmmm, maybe that wasn't my name.

I met Jo, my new mom, when she came home from a place called "work". She said that I was bigger than Max. Max? Who's Max? Is he the faded scent I smell in the house?

My dad explained to my mom that if he had not adopted me, I would be euthanized by now. My pawrents discussed going out to eat and buying me food and treats – which we eventually called "grocery shopping". My dad brought the crate into the house and placed it in the sun room. I didn't want to go in the crate. My dad tried to push me into the crate, but I spread my front legs so that I wouldn't fit in the opening. My dad was laughing, but I was serious – I didn't want to go in that crate. My pawrents talked and decided the master bathroom would be roomier and probably be more comfortable. They led me into a room smaller than the sun room, closed the door, and left the house.

No one answered when I whined. No one was in the house. I was in a room with two windows, but they were too high for me to see outside.

Keith was the first to return. He didn't go with my pawrents. He opened the door. He looked at me and looked around the room from the doorway. He told me that I'm in "trouble" and closed the door.

When my pawrents returned and opened the bathroom door, they appeared shocked. I did some redecorating and rearranging. I removed the curtains from the window next to the garden tub, pulled the mini blinds from the bathroom window next to a ceramic bowl that has water, and cleared everything from a counter with two empty water bowls. My pawrents said I destroyed the bathroom. My dad said sternly "Bad Boy!" I knew I did something wrong. I trembled, lowered my head, and peed where I sat. I was expecting to be hit, but no one hit me. My pawrents started cleaning the mess. They closed the door so I could not leave the room while they picked up the stuff. Their talking eventually led to laughter as they talked. I liked it when they started laughing. My dad invited me to sniff things as he put them back on the sink counter. I was cautious at first for fear of being hit with the objects. I started sniffing the objects and I liked the way he said "Good boy". I figured that I was helping. I watched him and my mom put the bathroom back into order – their kind of order. I realized that I wasn't going to get a beating, but I knew what I did was wrong. I never did that again! My dad and my mom never hit me. I'm in a family of nice hoomans!

After they cleaned up the bathroom, it was "supper time" – a phrase I learned very quickly. My dad emptied a can of food in a big dish – my very own supper dish! My dad called the can a "MRE" – meal ready-to-eat. I wanted to start eating, but my driver said "Wait." I didn't know what that meant, so I looked at him. He told me to "sit", but I didn't know what that meant. He helped me "sit". He said "wait" a few more times and said "Navy chow". What does that mean? What is "Navy" and what is this "chow" that he speaks of? He then said "Army chow" and said "OK" quickly and enthusiastically. I cocked my head at him, but didn't know what to do. He again said "Army chow – OK", so I cautiously went to my food dish. When he said "Good Boy", I knew he was happy with me. I chowed down and ate as quickly as I could. After I ate, my dad led me to the backyard on a leash and praised me when I went to the bathroom. That became our daily routine. But, for that night, that great meal gave me gas. I eventually learned that "Army chow" was always OK to eat, but not to eat anything that my dad calls "Navy chow". I didn't understand the reason, but that was OK with me.

A few days after being adopted – already a happy dog

How did I get my name? During my first night in my new home, my dad gave me a present. It was a foot-long thick thing he called a "raw hide" and "chew toy". I never had one before. I started chewing and chewing and chewing. When my dad and my mom went to sleep, I kept on chewing. Sometime during the night, I finished the raw hide. That was pretty good!

I went into the closet, found some leather, and chewed on that, too. It didn't taste good, so I stopped and left it in the closet. That leather thing was one of my mom's many shoes. The next morning, they found the shoe and were mad, but they didn't hit me. I understood the meaning of "Bad Boy!" and "No!" My dad searched for the raw hide, but could not find it. He asked me to find it – saying "Find your chew toy!" and "Where's your chew toy?" I sniffed around. I didn't know what he was talking about, so I didn't know what I was sniffing for. I just figured we lost something and he wanted me to help find it. After a while, he realized I chewed the entire raw hide. He couldn't believe I chewed the whole raw hide in one night! They started calling me "Chewy". By the afternoon, the raw hide was well digested and they talked about calling me "Stinky". After the shoe incident, I never chewed on anything, except raw hides and treats that my family gave me.

Tongue in the Wind

Chapter 2: Doctors and Healing

My dad took me to visit my doctor in Apex. Doc Bailey estimated my age at about 18 to 24 months. Doc Bailey and my dad decided to assume 18 months, which makes my birthday in a month called September. They chose the 15th as the day. Later, my pawrents decided to celebrate my birthday over a holiday called Labor Day weekend.

My dad thought I was a mix of Sheltie and Border Collie. Doc Bailey agreed that I probably had Collie in me. He said I was fortunate I didn't have the undercoat of a Sheltie. Doc Bailey was very gentle with me, talked to me in a calming voice, took some blood from me, and scheduled me to be "fixed". Doc Bailey told me that I have no idea how great of a life I will have with my dad. Yeah, but "fixed"? Why do hoomans tell me that I need fixing?

Before my procedure to be "fixed", I learned I had heart worms. I also had intestinal parasites, which probably caused my smelly gas problem. Well, maybe it was smelly to hoomans, but I was OK with it.

My dad was concerned about the heart worms. He told me that he didn't adopt me to put me to sleep. My dad and Doc Bailey arranged to start treating me with cyanide.

About a week after I was adopted, my driver was gone for two weeks. I waited for him, but he didn't come home. I don't know much about PTSD, but I learned quickly that I can comfort him. His medications seemed to be doing him more harm than good. He ended up in the hospital for almost two weeks after trying to end his life with no warning or indications. It was probably the medications. A doctor put him in a hospital for hoomans. The only pawson who could visit him was my mom. I had to stay home. I was confused. The man who rescued me and gave me lots of attention was gone. We're lucky that my mom came home unexpectedly, found my dad unconscious, dragged his body to the car, and took him to the hospital. She thought he died in the car. When my mom returned home, my dad wasn't with her. I sniffed for him, but couldn't find him. I was confused.

The medicine to treat my intestinal parasites caused me to have diarrhea. My mom put me in a very large crate when she went to work or went to visit my dad. One time, I couldn't hold the diarrhea and I went in my crate. My mom was almost sick from cleaning up the mess. She told me that was my dad's job, but he wasn't home. Where was my dad? I missed him. My mom seemed to understand what I was going through. That was the only time I ever messed in my crate.

I could smell my driver's scent on things, but I couldn't find him. About two weeks after my dad was absent in the house, my mom told me that she was going to get "Butchie". Butchie? What's a Butchie? You mean, my dad?!?! He's coming back?!?! I got excited sensing my mom's excitement.

Later in the day, my dad walked in the house. I wanted to jump on him, but I sensed something about him. I perked up my ears and wagged my tail. I went to him gently. He took me outside, and I sensed it was OK for me to go happy-crazy with him. The man who rescued me was back in my life! We sat together on the patio. He looked me straight in my eyes. He promised that he would never abandon me. He told me that if God called him Home, then God had a plan for me to be cared for and loved. He hugged me and cried. I put my muzzle against his cheek. He hugged me again and cried some more. I think he needed to cry, so I let him hug me and cry into my fur.

My dad took me back to Doc Bailey for a follow-up and to start my heart worm treatments. My weight was starting to climb, which was good. I wanted to run and play, but my dad wouldn't let me for three months until I was OK. We spent a lot of time lying on the floor together while he petted me and talked to me. He was the first pawson I ever trusted. My mom started referring to me as "shadow" because where ever my dad was, I was near him.

I watched my dad spend a lot of time in the garage working on a car called a "Cuda". We was either leaning forward and working on something on top of the motor, or underneath the car working on something. When he was underneath, I low crawled underneath to be next to him and to sniff what he was working on. My head would get grease from rubbing on things under the car. He explained how the car engine works. I pretended to be interested.

I wasn't sure what he was saying, but I liked his voice tone. If he removed something, he let me sniff it before he placed it on the ground or work bench. If he was installing a part, he let me sniff the part. A few months later, my dad sold the Cuda to a police officer. My pawrents needed the cash. My dad was home a lot because he couldn't work for a while. He wanted to work, but his doctors were trying to help him battle PTSD, which he later referred to as demons.

When Doc Bailey cleared me to be active again, my dad took me for walks on the Tobacco Trail near our house, which was in Apex, North Carolina. We walked slowly and every couple of days we increased the distance. I gradually regained my stamina and I could walk much faster and farther than my dad. I loved to run and trot and stop frequently to sniff all of the interesting scents on the trail. My dad sometimes jogged short distances with me, but he was out of shape and had back problems from an injury while he served in the US Army. My driver started riding his bicycle on the trail. That was pawfect because I could set the pace and he could keep up with me.

Here's a little bit about my dad. He might be out of shape now, but when was in the Army, he ran a lot. He loved to run miles and miles every day. He was one of the fastest runners in his units. He completed a marathon when he was a young lieutenant. One night many years before I came into his life, that all changed for him. He injured his upper back, and that injury eventually led to him leaving the Army. He didn't run much after that, and he's lucky to be walking.

My dad and I found some woods on public property that had a walking trail near the Cape Fear River. We started going there every Saturday. It was peaceful walking with my dad with only nature around us – and squirrels! Lots of squirrels! Squirrels were everywhere! I loved the game of chase that the squirrels played with me!

After a few trips to the trail, we noticed that we never saw anyone. I let my dad off our leash so he could walk at his own pace while I checked out all of the scents – and play chase with the squirrels! I would run ahead on the trail about 30-50 yards, then stop to look back. If I couldn't see my dad, I would back track on the trail to him, then run ahead of him again.

It didn't take long for us to invent a game. We called it hide-and-go-sniff. When I ran ahead of my dad, he would hide behind a tree or a tall clump of dirt and roots from an uprooted tree. When I stopped to look back and didn't see him, I would run back to where I last saw him. The first few times, I would run past where he was hiding. My dad would walk onto the trail when I was about 50 yards away and call my name. I would run back to him. It was pawrifically fun! I enjoyed being out there with him!

When we played hide-and-go-sniff, it wasn't long before I learned to stop at the location where I last saw him, then start sniffing the air and the ground. Soon, I was able to track him down no matter how far from the trail he hid. My dad gave me lots of praises for finding him and I loved playing that game. Sometimes, I would trick him. Instead of running out ahead 50 yards or so, I would stop at about 10-20 yards, then quickly look back. Sometimes, I caught my dad leaving the trail, and I would run to him and jump on his hip in excitement of catching him. I was getting good at keeping track of my dad! My mom went with us a few times, but she didn't hide. When my dad hid, I would go to my mom and pick up my dad's scent. My mom tried to trick me a few times. When my dad hid, my mom kept walking. I learned to run past her and find my dad's scent. Life was pawtastic with my pawrents! The bond between my dad and me grew stronger every week!

We played hide-and-go-sniff in the house, but with different rules. I would sit in the laundry room while my dad hid treats in different rooms of the house. Sometimes, if I thought he was taking too long or maybe he forgot to call me, I would slowly walk out of the laundry room and look for him. Regardless of whether I was looking for him or I was in the laundry room, when he said "OK", I knew it was time to sniff and find the treats. I pawsitively love my pawrents!

Chapter 3: Catching Wind

I don't like water, but my dad and I loved to sail. Pawsonally, I'm content just being with my dad. We had a trailerable sailboat with a cabin and two berths. Before adopting me, my pawrents had a Sheltie named Max. My dad and Max frequently camped on the boat and rode a jet ski together.

My dad and I did a lot of sailing. My first time on the sailboat was scary for me. My dad had to lead me to the sailboat and coax me to hop onto the boat and into the cockpit. Initially, I didn't like the rocking of the sailboat and being surrounded by water. I eventually became comfortable sitting in the cockpit while we moved slowly and quietly on the water. Whenever we sailed, my dad and I wore life jackets.

Chewy, a Sailing Dog

My first time on the sailboat, we had light winds. I chilled in the cockpit for a while and watched my driver pull this sheet and that sheet to make the boat change directions. He explained everything he was doing. He explained that sheets were ropes, and he let me sniff the sheets. I pretended to be interested, but some slow yawns would come out of me.

I discovered there were soft beds inside the cabin. The first time I went into the cabin, I curled up on the bed on the left side.

Hoomans had a funny name for things on the sailboat. I thought it was a bed, but my dad called it the port side berth or the starboard side berth. He peeked into the cabin and said "That's my berth! Your berth is on the starboard side." I liked the port side berth better, maybe because it had my dad's scent.

We had relaxing times. I enjoyed being with my dad. It was just God, my dad and me. My dad used the time to connect with God. He talked with God and used His winds to take us places on the lake.

On one of my sailing days, it was hot. My dad dropped an anchor in the water and jumped into the water with his life jacket on. He kept calling me to jump in, but I don't like water. My dad climbed into the sailboat, lowered me into the water with my doggie life jacket, and he jumped into the water again. I swam and swam around him. I tried to climb on him to get out of the water. My dad tried to show me how to float and trust the life jacket, but I didn't like being in the water. After about 30 minutes in the water, I realized I was floating with my dad and didn't have to doggie paddle.

We floated together and he talked with me. When he climbed aboard, I thought he was going to leave me. As he climbed onto the ladder, my paw grabbed his swim trunks and pulled them down to his ankles. I was blinded by his bright, white tushy and I left a claw mark on his right rump. I swam around the boat trying to figure out how to climb aboard. I wanted to climb the ladder but I couldn't figure out how to reach my paws up to it. My dad called me over to the side of the boat. He kept calling to me and I eventually swam to him. I reckon by then I was looking desperate. He reached down, grabbed the loop handle on top of my life jacket, and lifted me into the cockpit. That was easy! Why didn't he tell me that before I started getting desperate?

On another sailing trip, we drove about two hours to a place called Kerr Lake. It is a much larger lake. The weather forecast was for clear skies and breezy – perfect for a day on the water. We arrived early in the morning. It was still dark. By the time we raised the mast and put the boat in the water, the sky was starting to turn an orange color on the horizon. The water was calm and there was no breeze, so my dad used the motor for a few minutes.

He then shut it off, turned on the radio, got a bucket and brush from the storage bin under the tiller, filled the bucket with water, and started scrubbing the cockpit. Our sailboat had a self-bailing cockpit, so the water always flowed out. I went into the cabin to get out of his way and to take a nap.

I heard the water lapping against the hull and I heard my dad yell "Chewy, we've got a breeze!" I climbed into the cockpit and sat with my dad as we sailed along slowly. Later in the morning, the winds picked up and there were waves about 12 to 18 inches. I went into the cabin. The sailboat heeled and I heard and felt the bow slam into the waves. The boat was rocking! I got sick and vomited all over my dad's berth. I climbed out of the cabin and into the cockpit. I vomited inside the cockpit. My dad told me to hang on for about 30 minutes. He was headed to an island in the lake. He sailed to the leeward side (the side opposite the wind) and dropped the anchor. He used the bucket to wash my vomit out of the cockpit. He went into the cabin and sat on a wet spot. He realized I vomited on his berth. He cleaned it up and asked if I was OK. Then he said "Let's eat lunch." Eat? Did he say eat? I perked my ears and tilted my head left and right.

While we ate lunch on the leeward side of the island, my dad and I could see the waves getting taller. There were these things he called white caps. He taught me that meant we need to be more careful.

After lunch, he closed the cabin hatch and he pointed the boat towards the general direction of the boat ramp. It took us about three hours to sail to this island, but he figured we would make better time going back to the boat ramp. We moved slowly at first, then the sails caught the wind and the boat heeled. My dad adjusted the mainsail and jib. The boat was moving faster than I had ever experienced. I looked over the side several times, and each time my face was splashed with water. The winds were strong. My dad said "Chewy, I think we need to reef the mainsail and lower the jib." At about that time, a strong gust caught our sails. The boat was leaning heavy to the port side. I clawed on the fiberglass to climb to the starboard side, but I kept slipping. My dad was holding onto a cleat with one hand, the tiller with the other and was standing on the side of the cockpit seat. He slowly turned

15

into the wind and the boat returned to an angle in which I could climb to my dad. When I reached him, a stronger gust caught our sails and the boat felt like it was going to flip over. Water came over the bow and hit our faces. Then, lots of water poured over the gunnel into the cockpit. It seemed like the cockpit completely filled with water in less than two seconds. My dad let go of the tiller. The boat pointed itself into the wind and became upright as it did. My dad waded to the top of the cabin and held onto the mast. I swam in the cockpit to join him and he helped me onto the top of the cabin. He looked at me with a huge smile. He was whoopin' and hollerin' and laughin'. I gave him a crazy look. We were both soaked, the cockpit was full of water, the waves were rocking us, and he's having a good time? Is he nuts? As the water slowly flowed through two drain tubes in the back of the cockpit, my dad told me "Chewy, you're the Skipper! It's a good thing the cabin hatch is closed, or you'd have to go down with your ship!"

When the cockpit was empty of water, he let the boat's sails keep us pointed into the wind. He showed me how to reef the mainsail. He couldn't do the same to the jib, so he lowered the jib. After about 10 minutes, we were ready to continue sailing to the boat ramp. It took us much longer, but I felt safer. My dad started singing a song. I think he made up the words, but it went something like this. "99 leather-bound Bibles on the wall. 99 leather-bound Bibles. Give one away. Jesus will save. 98 Bibles left on the wall. 98 leather-bound Bibles on the wall. 98 leather-bound Bibles. Give one away. Jesus will save. 97 Bibles left on the wall..." Does this song ever end? I think he got to about 40-something and we sailed into a leeward area where the land was blocking the wind and reduced it to a nice breeze. Rather than raising the sails, my driver cranked up the outboard motor. I tilted my head and looked at the motor, then looked at him. Now, why didn't he do that to begin with? We had more than enough fuel to travel from the island to the boat ramp! I learned that with my dad, it's all about the adventure and trusting God during the journey.

We putted for about 20 minutes to the boat ramp. We were on the leeward side of the land and trees, so the water had ripples. We could see towards the center of the lake that conditions had worsened. I hopped on the cabin and stood on the bow. My dad steered the boat left and right to try to help me lose my balance. By now, I learned how to balance myself on my sailboat. I must be a good saildog because my dad called me "Skipper". He told me "Aye Aye, Skipper" after asking me a question. Like, "Cruise along the shoreline? Aye Aye, Skipper!" and "Turn 30 degrees starboard? Aye Aye, Skipper!"

It takes us about an hour to put the sailboat on the trailer, remove and stow the sails, and lower and secure the mast, boom and sheets. I laid in the shadow of the boat and supawvised my dad as he sang and talked to me. I howled with him because he sings way out of tune and it bothers my ears! I'm glad no one was around, because they would think my dad is nuts. It's a good thing he doesn't sing for a living!

On the drive home, I slept soundly in the backseat. I would wake up after mumbling and sleep-barking softly, and my dad would ask if I had good sailing dreams. It was hard for me to perk up my ears, but I would try briefly, then fall asleep again.

Tongue in the Wind

Chapter 4: First Ride

I had been with my pawrents for about three years when we moved to another house. We moved to the country near a place called Kipling, about 15 minutes south of a small town called Fuquay Varina, North Carolina. My dad, and a few hoomans, refers to Fuquay Varina as "The Quay" or "The Kway."

My dad and my mom purchased a Harley-Davidson Electra Glide Ultra Classic in the summer. My dad rode street motorcycles since he was 15. He loved to ride. It gave him a temporary escape from PTSD demons.

After my dad broke his back in the Army, he struggled everyday with upper back and neck pain. My dad had a Honda Gold Wing motorcycle, but he sold it before adopting me. When he sold the bike, he had not planned on buying another. It didn't take long for him to realize that riding was therapeutic for him. Riding stimulates his senses and keeps him in the present. My mom encouraged him to buy a bike. I think he was becoming a pain in her butt as he battled demons. But, instead of a Gold Wing, they bought the Harley-Davidson. I knew when it fired up that dad and mom would be gone most of the day. I would have to stay at home and wait for them.

A few months after buying the Harley-Davidson, my mom had vertebras fused in her lower back. The orthopedic surgeon told her she would never ride again. They asked the doctor about a side car, but the doctor explained that the lack of support and the rough ride of a motorcycle or side car could injure her back.

My dad rode solo for several months. I wasn't afraid of the bike. When my dad returned home, I could hear the bike before he was on our street. My mom would let me in the front yard. If my dad saw me in the yard, he would pass the house and I would run after him. He would turn around, and I would run with him back to the house. Every time I raced my dad, I would win!

A few times, my dad let me sit on the driver seat, then fire up the bike. I kind of understood the relationship between my dad and that bike. To him, riding was a temporary escape from the demons. Maybe the couple of years of not having a bike before adopting me kind of led to a downward spiral in his battle with those demons, and that's why he was becoming a pain in my mom's butt.

My first ride was in mid-Spring. I had been with my pawrents for four years, and I was about five and half years old, in hooman years.

A large box arrived at our home. It was a custom motorcycle dog seat. The owner of the company that made the seat told my dad that he should set the seat near my dog dish for a week so that I become familiar with it. My dad opened the box and removed the seat from the box. He sat the seat in the middle of the living room, then read the papers. While he read, I sniffed the seat. After several minutes of reading, my dad noticed my curiosity. The seat was made of leather with two-inch shearling lining the inside. My dad talked to me and let me know it was OK to get in the seat, so I did. I made myself comfortable and sniffed the seat's interior while sitting in it. He then told me "Hmmmm. I wonder what you'll do if I let you watch me mount that seat on the bike." I followed him into the garage. There are two straps that secure the seat to the passenger saddle. I sniffed the straps before he put the seat on the bike.

It took my dad over an hour to figure out how to mount my seat on the bike. After my dad seemed satisfied that my seat was secured, he went into the house to fetch my new goggles. I stayed in the garage looking at the seat. When he returned to the garage about a minute or two later, I was in my seat. I figured out how to mount the bike and plop myself in my seat.

My dad helped me dismount. He wanted me to follow him into the house, but I kept stopping and looking at the bike. He told me it was OK, and that I had to wear a safety harness. He put a harness on me and adjusted it. After several minutes, I followed him to the bedroom. He went into the closet, grabbed his helmet, boots, gloves, and riding glasses. At about that time, my mom came home. My dad put on his boots, and then I followed him to the garage. Once in the garage, I immediately went to the bike and hopped into my seat.

My dad connected three retainer straps to my harness. He put goggles on my face and adjusted the straps. My mom couldn't believe what she was seeing. My dad gave the camera to my mom. My mom and dad were both smiling at me. I was calm.

Preparing for my first ride

My dad put on his helmet and gloves, mounted my Harley-Davidson, fired her up, and we rolled slowly out of the garage. In the driveway, he dismounted and checked my harness. I sat calmly in the seat as the H-D massaged me with its vibration. My dad mounted the H-D and rolled her onto the street. We rode slowly. This was better than putting my head out of a car window – and much better than sailing!

The first ride

We rode up and down the street several times before my dad noticed we needed gas. When we passed our house, my mom took pictures of us. Riding with my dad was soooo pawesome!

We rolled onto the driveway and he shut down the bike. He told me that he needed to fuel up the bike. I think he was planning to ride solo to get fuel. He disconnected my harness and tried to coax me out of the seat. He gave me a taste of riding and I wasn't getting out of my seat! I hunkered down into the seat. I was NOT dismounting!

My dad reconnected my harness. That was more like it! My dad mounted the bike and backed her onto the street. We rolled out of our neighborhood onto a country road. We rode somewhat slowly at about 30-35 mph so we could both get comfortable. My dad became my driver! How pawrific is that?

We rode to a gas station in a small town called Duncan, which is about 10-12 minutes from our house. He eventually accelerated to about 40-45 mph. I leaned out slightly and put my face in the wind. Yup, this was better than riding in a car! More importantly, I was with my dad, uh, I mean, driver!

We stopped in Duncan for gas. I sat in my seat and watched my driver so I could learn the refuel routine. After refueling, we took the "long" way home down country roads. We rode about 40-45 mph, and occasionally would go 50-55. When we returned home, my mom said I was soooo cool, but she had difficulty believing that I was actually riding. My driver backed the H-D onto the street again, and we rode on our neighborhood streets.

That was a pawsome day! After we parked the H-D in the garage, I didn't want to dismount. My driver tried to help me, but I hunkered down into the seat. My driver closed the garage door and went into the house. A few minutes later, he returned. I was still in my seat. He coaxed me for several minutes to dismount. When I realized we weren't going to ride, I stepped out of my saddle, and hopped onto the garage floor. Afterwards, each time my driver went into the garage, I followed him and I jumped onto the bike and stepped into my seat.

My driver eventually helped me to understand that he did not want me jumping onto the bike. His primary concern was the hot pipes and engine burning me if I slipped from the driver's seat.

When I'm mounted on my Harley-Davidson, it is very calming for me. I sit directly behind my driver and I love riding with him.

We rode almost every day after my driver returned from work. I quickly learned the signs of getting ready to ride. He wears jeans when he is around the house, but I learned that he only wears boots when he is going to ride. After a few days, we became comfortable riding together at highway speeds. I enjoyed putting my tongue in the wind!

Tongue in the Wind

Chapter 5: First Group Rides

My first group ride was a couple of weeks after my first ride. Instead of going to Church that morning, my driver took me on a 45-minute ride to Jordan Lake. I trusted <u>my</u> hoomans, but I was still afraid of hoomans. My driver wasn't sure how I was going to react around lots of hoomans, or how hoomans would react to me. We were both starting a lot of first-time things together.

My first goggles

When we arrived at Jordan Lake, there were lots of motorcycles participating in the Pediatric Brain Tumor Foundation's Ride for Kids. As a member of Raleigh H.O.G., my driver parked with that group. Each year, the group that raises the most funds leads the ride the following year. Raleigh H.O.G. was leading the ride because they raised the most funds the previous year. I met many new friends, including Steve and Janet. Steve was the Director of the Raleigh H.O.G. chapter.

We climbed the hill to register for the event. I sniffed a lot of places during the short walk. At the registration area, we received a lot of looks and double takes. Most of the hoomans who talked with my driver assumed I rode in a side car. I was timid, but I cautiously and curiously sniffed hoomans as they talked with my driver. Hoomans gave me pieces of donuts and biscuits. I learned quickly that hoomans who smell like the road are probably bikers like my driver. Bikers are nice to me! This was good therapawy for me! I was having a great expawrience and learning that hoomans around bikes are nicest hoomans I could ever meet.

The riders gathered for a safety briefing. After the prayer, it was time to ride! That was my first group prayer! I was a bit excited and I jumped into my seat instead of waiting for my driver to lift me. He put my goggles on me. Then, I heard hundreds of motorcycles fire up. Since we were riding with Raleigh H.O.G., I could only hear the rumble of lots of Harley-Davidsons that were around me. I looked around at a sea of the hoomans on their bikes. There were hoomans on bikes everywhere I looked! This was really pawesome!

The ride was escorted by Chatham County Sheriff's Department and we rode around Jordan Lake. It was a scenic ride that lasted over an hour. I think the procession of bikes stretched several miles. We rode into Pittsboro, rode around the circle in the center of town, and rode out the same way we came in. Bikes were rolling southbound and northbound. Bikers were waving at each other and honking their horns. We never saw the end of the bikes when we turned onto US Highway 64 a couple of miles from the center of town.

When we returned to Jordan Lake, we dismounted and my driver gave me some water. On the previous night, he froze a large bottle of water for me so that I would have cold water as it thawed. Freezing a bottle of water became routine for us.

It was time for lunch during the event's Celebration of Life. I shared a ham sandwich with my driver. Other bikers shared parts of their sandwiches with me. This was a doggie's dream!

I was tired when we returned home, but I was happy. I spent nearly the whole day with my driver, met lots of nice hoomans, and they shared food with me.

My next group ride was a week later. My driver and I rode to Ray Price Harley-Davidson (RPHD) in Raleigh to ride with Raleigh H.O.G., led by Steve. Mr. Price was going to fly in a World War II airplane at an airfield north of Raleigh. While at

RPHD, I was allowed into the dealership. I met Ms. Jean (Mr. Price's wife) and some of the dealership staff. Most had already heard about me from the Ride for Kids on the previous weekend. I quickly learned where they kept the donuts and cookies. I also learned that everyone in the dealership is friendly. It did not take long for me to understand that bikers won't hurt me. They are the friendliest hoomans I ever met during my lifetime. One of the dealership staffers named Ms Amy was nice to me and she started keeping treats at her desk for me. Whenever I visited the dealership, I led my driver straight to Ms Amy's desk!

So, back to the ride.

The H.O.G. group rode to a restaurant for breakfast. Everyone went into the restaurant, including my driver. I had to stay outside. I explored the porch, which had a few chairs. After a few minutes, my driver came out with a white container. I'm glad he came outside to be with me. I didn't understand why I couldn't go inside the building. He and I ate breakfast on the porch. It was good. Steve checked on us a few times to ask if I needed water or more bacon. Bacon? Did Steve say "bacon"? He brought some bacon to me. I like Steve!

After eating, we went for a short stroll around the parking lot. Soon, the rest of the group came out of the restaurant. We mounted up to ride to the airport.

At the airport, we were allowed to park on the tarmac. There were two World War II trainers. I was OK with the loud engines and propeller noise. As the day grew hotter, my driver kept me in the shade under the wing of a plane. I was accustomed to the temperature, but my paws weren't accustomed to the heat of the tarmac. I drank lots of cold water. My frozen water in a half-gallon jug slowly thawed in the saddlebag, so I had ice cold water to drink.

On this trip, my driver started exposing me to cameras. My initial reaction with cameras was uncertainty and fear – my ears go back and I lower my head. My driver let me sniff the camera and helped me to understand that neither the camera nor the flash of light from the camera would hurt me.

Over the next several weeks, we rode frequently. We were becoming accustomed to hoomans drifting into our traffic lane when they saw us on four-lane roads. I don't think it's intentional. Most of the hoomans can look at us and drive at the same time, but there are a few who try to take pictures while driving, or talking on a cell phone while driving and looking at us. Those hoomans would drift towards us, so my driver would decelerate so that we would not ride off the road as the car drifted towards us. My driver became more defensive in his driving.

Chapter 6: Flash

Our first night ride was interesting.

We were riding back roads around The Kway. After the sun dropped in the horizon, we headed back into The Kway. At a stop light, we were idling and listening to music. I was chillin'. Suddenly, there was a flash of light on our right. I saw my driver quickly turn his head to the right. Then, a flash to our left. I could sense that my driver was becoming uncomfortable. I was uncertain with what was happening. I leaned against his back and snuggled my muzzle against his neck. We realized that hoomans were taking pictures beside us and behind us.

Later, my driver and I told Steve about the hoomans taking pictures. Steve called them "puppy"-razzis. He told us to get used to it. He was right. Several times of the years, Steve told us that I might by the most photographed pup in North Carolina.

Tongue in the Wind

Chapter 7: Honoring our Fallen

By June, most of my rides were on back roads in Harnett County and southern Wake County. My driver talked with me about going to a HOG rally in Salisbury, North Carolina. That would be my longest distance ride so far. We joined a group from Raleigh H.O.G. on a day trip. We learned a lot on this ride. The ride itself was great. When the H.O.G. members went to a restaurant, my driver didn't want to leave me in the heat while he went into an air-conditioned restaurant. We stayed at the rally and shared hot dogs and chips and sniffed the various vendors. We had a relaxing time, but this taught us to plan for meals on long rides. It was a hot, long day. When we returned home, my driver gave me a cool bath, then he took a shower. We both slept good and snored.

My driver prayed as to whether or not to bring me to a Patriot Guard mission. I just want to ride where he rides. I do my best to be well-behaved. My first mission with the Patriot Guard Riders (PGR) was at the Fayetteville airport in the middle of summer. Two heroes were returning home: one via Pope Air Force Base, the other via Fayetteville airport. PGR members were planned to be at both locations. My driver and I were the first to arrive at Fayetteville airport. I sniffed and greeted the family, honor guard, and my new PGR brothers as they arrived.

About six PGR members were at Fayetteville airport, and there were about ten or so at Pope AFB. The aircraft landed first at Pope Air Base. There was a delay. During the delay, I sat with some of the family members when they came outside of the building to wait. About 30 minutes later, the aircraft was cleared to make the short hop to Fayetteville.

Army Master Sergeant Shawn Simmons arrived. The PGR and an Honor Guard from the 82nd Airborne Division stood at attention. I sat at attention in the shade of my driver. After the flag-draped casket was lowered from the Kalitta Charters aircraft, I saw Mrs. Simmons put her hand on the casket. Their two children where with her. Something was wrong with my driver. I had never sensed him like this. My driver was standing at attention with tears streaming down his face. I moved to lean against his left leg and put my paw on his left boot. He looked down at me. I looked up at him. I didn't make any noise. I sensed something different about him. It wasn't the same as when he has flashbacks. We hadn't trained me in how to react to this type of emotion. I leaned against his leg and gently licked his left hand to try to comfort him while he stood at attention.

Once the casket was in the hearse, we quickly mounted the bikes. Cumberland County Sheriff's Deputies were leading the procession to the funeral home, followed by the motorcycles and the hearse. At the funeral home, more PGR members were waiting. We dismounted and formed an honor line. Some PGR members saluted and others put their right hand over their heart as our Fallen Hero was moved from the hearse and into the funeral home. My driver saluted.

The senior military officer, a lieutenant colonel, shook the hands of each PGR member and thanked them for what they do. I sat to the right of my driver. The officer patted me on the head. I raised my paw and shook his hand. I think the officer was impressed with my behavior and my display of honor and respect. I think the PGR members were also impressed with my conduct.

After my driver and I returned home from my first PGR mission, my driver and I sat on the floor in the bonus room. He prayed a lot and asked God to help him and to give him guidance. My driver petted me, and sometimes he buried his face in my fur while he prayed. He told me that he thinks that God put me in his life to bring comfort to hoomans, not just to him. We spent most of the night in the bonus room.

By the end of the summer, we were averaging over 1,000 miles per month.

Chapter 8: The Lump

I had been riding for five months when I attended my first Ray Price Capital City BikeFest, which is always the last weekend in September. The BikeFest is in downtown Raleigh. This is a family-oriented event and one of the first events in which Raleigh closed Fayetteville Street for a weekend event.

There were bikes of all kinds and hoomans of all kinds, not just bikers. The BikeFest is a weekend event that starts on Friday. My driver and I volunteered to help at the event.

On Friday, we poured free soda drinks. Next, we participated in the annual Patriot Ride, which benefited organizations such as the North Carolina National Guard. On Saturday, we spent the day at the prize booth at Ray Price H-D. I slept while my driver manned the table.

In downtown Raleigh, Raleigh H.O.G. had a table where they sold raffle tickets for a Harley-Davidson motorcycle. All of the proceeds from the raffle go to various charities. The Raleigh H.O.G. table was on the far end away from the bike entrance. There wasn't as much traffic in the area of the table.

When the dealership closed for the day and our volunteer shift ended, we rode to Fayetteville Street. While parking, dozens of hoomans were snapping pictures of me. My driver and I dismounted and started walking. Steve came to us and asked if we could help draw hoomans to the H.O.G. table. We weren't sure how to help, but Steve already had an idea. He told us to mount up and follow him. While we put on our helmets, Steve cleared it with traffic control for us to ride our Harley-Davidson to the H.O.G. table. We pulled out of our parking space. We followed Steve as he walked down Fayetteville Street. Dozens of hoomans, or maybe about a hundred, seemed to be following us, pointing at us, and taking pictures. Most of them followed us to the H.O.G. table, where we parked. My driver dismounted, but I stayed in my seat so hoomans could take pictures. We now had a crowd near the H.O.G. table, and it was up to the H.O.G. members to sell tickets. We stayed there for about three hours. I took a 15 minute break every 15 minutes. I liked being in my seat because that is when most of the hoomans would approach me, let me sniff their hands, and pet me. I didn't mind as long as I could see my driver. Since the money raised from the bike raffle goes to multiple charities in the area, I hope I did a good job in drawing hoomans to the raffle table. I continued learning that bikers are friendly hoomans.

After BikeFest, my driver and I began researching if I could become a member of H.O.G. He found no rules that excluded dogs. Our logic was that the average biker rides about 3,000 miles/year, depending upon the source. We estimated that I was on the path to ride over 12,000 miles/year. Several members of Raleigh H.O.G. encouraged my driver to submit an application for my membership. With the amount of rubber we were putting on the road together, a H.O.G. membership seemed justified. That research took a back seat when my mom found a lump in her breast.

My mom survived breast cancer 21 years earlier and had a mastectomy. She found a new lump and asked my dad to feel it. I sensed they were both worried. I wanted to hop onto the bed and sniff the lump, but my driver wouldn't let me. I was curious as to what they were feeling.

The oncologist estimated the mass at about one centimeter. He obtained a tissue sample. From what I'm told, my driver passed out while watching them remove the sample.

My mom preferred a mastectomy rather than a lumpectomy. The day before surgery, my driver checked me into Camp Bow Wow, anticipating that I would be there for several days while my mom was in the hospital. I didn't understand what was going on. I only knew that my pawrents were very worried. Days before I checked into Camp Bow Bow, my driver didn't want my mom to see him with me. We would sit upstairs in the bonus room together and he would bury his face in my fur and cry. I didn't know what to do except to snuggle against him, and gently lick his hand and chin.

Immediately after surgery, the surgeon talked with my driver. He explained that the mass had grown to about three centimeters in about four weeks, so my mom's choice of a mastectomy was the right decision. A biopsy would later find that another mass on the other side of her breast was undetected, which reconfirmed that my mom's decision for a mastectomy was correct. My mom is a smart cookie! (Did I say "cookie"? I like cookies.)

By comparison, the easy part was over. While my mom recovered from surgery, my driver submitted my application for H.O.G. membership. In late Fall, I became an associate member of H.O.G., then joined Raleigh H.O.G. I was about six years old.

The next year would be a tough year. My mom began chemotherapy at the beginning of the year, and it lasted many months.

During her first chemo treatment, she had a bad reaction. My driver was scared because they rushed the "crash cart" to her. When they returned home that evening, I could sense that mom was tired. My driver was emotionally drained.

My driver talked with me later and prayed. When my mom was crashing and they were rushing the cart to her, the staff told my driver to keep talking to my mom. My driver was on his knees, held her hand and talked to her through his tears. He stayed on his knees while the staff worked on my mom. My dad may seem stoic (I learned that word from listening to others) on the outside, but he loves my mom very much. While my mom slept, my driver and I went upstairs to pray. He prayed that my mom and my dad were like second lieutenants in the Army and interchangeable. He asked God that if it was my mom's time to go, to please take him, let my mom stay with me, and to take care of my mom and me.

After nearly losing my mom, rather than a treatment every four weeks, my mom received a chemo treatment every week with a different drug. Over the weeks, my mom grew weaker and lost her hair. It was tough on my mom, but it was also tough on my driver trying to take care of her, work about 75-80 hours/week in his job, and travel (sometimes to other countries). Many times, my mom laid on the couch and I would sit next to her on the floor. She would pet me and cry. I wish I could do more to comfort her.

It snowed one day, and my mom wanted to see the snowman her grandkids made. My driver came home early that day – he probably had a late night international teleconference coming up. My mom was depressed and I couldn't comfort her. My driver decided to take us to hamburger place, then see the grandkids. My mom and I jumped in the car. She didn't want to be seen in public, so we ate in the car. Getting my mom out of the house for dinner and seeing the snow was good for her. We went to visit the grandkids and looked at their snowman. For someone battling for her life, that simple "date" was a bright spot. I'm happy that I was able to be part of it.

Over the next several months, my mom slept a lot. My driver was worried about her and spent a lot of time in the upstairs bonus room to pray. When he knelt on the floor, I would lay next to him, if I wasn't downstairs with my mom laying next to the couch or the bed. I may not understand God, Jesus, and praying, but I do know that it gave my driver strength to take care of my mom and to keep working full time. We rode the Harley-Davidson when we could, but we were riding much less than 1,000 miles/month.

My mom finished chemo before summer. Emotionally, she felt better, but she was physically weak.

We don't like that "c" word.

Chapter 9: Texas

My driver had a high school reunion coming up in the middle of summer after my mom completed chemotherapy. My mom encouraged him to go. My driver doesn't remember much about high school and childhood. I think it's part of the demons he battles. He remembers a few friends and the family dog, Ladd. Ladd rode a motorcycle with my driver when my driver was a teenager!

My mom and my driver talked about flying my mom to Corpus Christi, Texas to meet us, but the doctor said it was risky because of her suppressed immunity. She didn't have the energy or strength to follow in the cage, and they talked about putting me at Camp Bow Wow and driving together. My mom didn't have the strength to sit in a car for six or seven days. My mom's mom lived about three minutes away, and Matt, their oldest son (one of my hooman brothers), lived about 15 minutes away. We had family that could check-in on my mom. My mom encouraged my driver to go to Texas – and to bring me with him!

My driver began planning the road trip to Kingsville. I would be going to South Texas with him! We learned quickly that finding a hotel that accepts dogs was difficult. We also learned that many pet-friendly hotels that we found also have restrictions on the size of the pets.

Travelling with me on a motorcycle requires more planning than travelling in a car. With the trip being in the summer, I don't have clothes to pack, but I do have food that needs to be packed. Finding pet stores along the way would slow us down and my driver won't leave me in a store parking lot on a hot summer day.

My driver found a few pet-friendly hotels along our route, but he could not find a pet-friendly hotel in Kingsville. We also found no kennels in Kingsville. The only dog boarding we could find in Kingsville was veterinarian offices, but none would be open on Sunday morning when my driver and I wanted to begin our return to North Carolina. My driver found a kennel outside of Odem, which was near Beeville where my driver's parents were living. My driver did not want to leave me with his parents. My driver made reservations, sent a copy of my vaccination records, and we were set.

Two days before hitting the road, my driver began packing. I sensed he was excited about something, but I wasn't exactly sure what he was up to. When I saw him pack eight cans of my food, a large zip lock bag of my dry food, and my treats, I knew something was up. Would I be going to my doggie hotel? I watched him pack my food in the same bag as his cloths. I sniff checked the bags frequently. My driver said that my consumables would be replaced by souvenir T-shirts during our ride. Ride? Did he say "ride"? I understand that hooman word!

On a morning in mid-summer, my driver said a short prayer. We saddled up and fired up the engine. The sun had been up for about an hour. My mom took a picture of us, told us to be careful, and to have fun. This was a good day for a ride! The bike felt heavier. We had a travel bag on the luggage rack. In the travel bag was a small ice chest and some of my food. This bag blocked most of my view to the rear. I don't know where Texas is, but that didn't matter. I was with my driver!

Ready to roll to Texas

My driver and mom agreed that my driver would send a text message at almost every stop. This would let my mom know that we are OK and also let her know our location.

Our first planned stop was at the Harley-Davidson dealership in Hickory, North Carolina. We had incorrectly assumed that dogs who are card-carrying H.O.G. members would be allowed in dealerships. We respected their rule, so I stayed under a tree while my driver used their restroom. We chatted briefly with one of the mechanics outside, then hit the highway.

Our next planned dealership stop was the Harley-Davidson dealership in Waynesville. We weren't sure if they would be pet friendly. We quickly found they were very pet friendly. We met a new friend, Fred from Ohio. I think Fred was headed south with friends.

Our planned route to Knoxville, Tennessee would take us on a scenic route on Tail of the Dragon, a section of US highway 129 in North Carolina and Tennessee. Tail of the Dragon is known for having 318 curves in 11 miles. This was the first time I was in this part of North Carolina, and the scenery and roads were totally pawesome. We stopped a few times enroute to Deals Gap to sniff the area while my driver simply looked at the scenery. It smelled and looked beautiful! This area would become our favorite riding area in North Carolina.

When we arrived at Deals Gap, the store staff told my driver that I couldn't be in the store. Someone in the store asked if I was the dog who was riding on the Harley. Once they realized that I rode in, they let me in the store so we could buy a T-shirt. We were at Deals Gap for about an hour. I sniffed a lot of hoomans and liked everyone I sniffed.

Tail of the Dragon was strange. We somehow fell into a group of about 30 crotch rockets that were going faster than my driver's comfort. He counter-steered left and right, so I was either looking at sky and treetops, or watching the pavement come up to me. For the first mile or so, I squirmed in my seat when I saw pavement. A few times, I heard the scraping sound of our floorboards on the pavement. I know my driver could feel me shifting as the bike leaned left and right. I vomited on the right saddlebag. We stopped on a shoulder to let the bikers behind us pass. I offered to lick up my mess, but my driver used some of the water we carried to rinse it off. He was laughing the whole time and calling me "po' Chewy". He took off my helmet and goggles and rubbed my head. Enough of that – let's ride!

With no bikers behind us, we cruised at a more comfortable speed to enjoy the scenery, stopping at a stone wall so I could spend an hour leaving pee-mail. My driver looked at the scenery and talked with a couple during their Christian mission of providing free tea, lemonade and water, and ministering to hoomans.

Tail of the Dragon, US129, North Carolina

We had reservations at a dog-friendly hotel in Knoxville, but we weren't sure how to get there. We only knew it was on I-40. We still had plenty of daylight, so we rode and enjoyed the scenery. We found I-140 and hopped on it. When we reached I-40, we traveled west. When we reached the I-40/I-75 split, we realized we were going the wrong way. We exited and returned on I-40 heading east. The hotel was only a couple of miles from where we had originally hopped onto I-40.

We arrived at the hotel at about 6pm. My driver unloaded the bike while I dragged my leash around and checked and left pee-mail on bushes. We had a large king room on the ground floor.

What's for dinner? The person at the front desk told us about a number of restaurants, but none were pet-friendly. My driver was craving a sammich. We hopped on the bike to refuel and hopefully find a fast-food restaurant nearby. We found a sammich shop. I stayed outside while my driver bought our dinner. He got an Italian-style sammich for himself, and a 6-inch meatball sub for me. When he came out, I knew one of the sammiches was for me! I was alternating lifting my left and right front paws off the ground in excitement while licking my lips! We mounted up and went back to the hotel to eat. After my sub sammich, I had my regular dinner, a can of my MRE (Meal, Ready to Eat – it's a military thing). We kept our routine of going outside after my dinner. My driver took a long shower while I took a nap. We both crashed early and my driver woke me up a few times because I was snoring. We were tired, but we were feeling good.

We were up before sunrise. We wanted to get through Memphis, Tennessee before evening rush hour, so we got an early start. We got onto I-40 eastbound, and quickly realized we were going in the wrong direction. We exited and headed westbound. It was cool that morning and the scenery was beautiful. We stopped about every hour to stretch, walk, and warm up a little.

We stopped at the Harley-Davidson dealership in Nashville, and I posed with the RCA dog. I sniffed him, but he didn't return the sniff. He just sat there with his head cocked and ears up, so I imitated him. Hoomans in the dealership were taking pictures of me. The hooman word "cute" was said a lot.

Somewhere west of Nashville, we rolled into a rest area so we could stretch our legs and empty our bladders. When we returned to the bike, a man started talking with us. His family was standing behind him. He asked us the usual questions, like "Where you headed?", "Where'd you come from?", and "Does that dog really ride?" He told us that there were forecasts for thunderstorms and we would probably run into some rain on our way to Memphis.

"What do you when it rains?" the man asked.

"Get wet" replied my driver.

The man looked at his family, pointed to us, and said "Now, THAT's the real deal."

The "real deal"? Lots of bikers get wet when it rains. The ones with a bit more sense than us will stop to put on rain gear. But, on hot days with scattered showers, my driver and I prefer to roll through it because when we get to the other side, we'll dry off quickly.

Nashville, Tennessee

About an hour east of Memphis, it was noticeably hotter. We stopped at an office building in Memphis. This must be the place that my driver visits when his job takes him to Memphis. A friendly lady named Madonna gave me a tour of the office suite. I sniffed around, and became very interested in the break room. We visited the office for about 30 minutes, and hoomans took pictures of me.

After leaving the office, we took a short ride and stopped at a Harley-Davidson retail shop for a T-shirt. They were friendly. We took lots of pictures. I was just happy to be in air conditioning again and I laid down while my driver shopped. Woof of approval for being biker doggie friendly.

There were a lot of trucks between Memphis and Little Rock. The traffic speed fluctuated a lot. We arrived in Little Rock about an hour before sundown, ordered a pizza, and we crashed.

We were up well before sunrise to get a jump on the heat to San Antonio. My driver said a prayer, thanked the Lord, and we were rolling before sunrise.

Shortly after sunrise south of Little Rock, a gray pickup truck passed us on the left lane. They slowed down, then sped up, then slowed down again. The person in the passenger seat started throwing empty cans at us. My driver decelerated. The truck decelerated, and a glass bottle came at us. My driver put the bike onto the shoulder of the interstate and decelerated. Another bottle came towards us and shattered on the pavement. The truck decelerated and drifted towards us. My driver accelerated hard while on the shoulder and moved the bike to the right lane. He could see the truck catching up from behind. The pickup moved to the left lane. We were coming up on an exit. My driver stayed in the lane and accelerated. I wasn't ready for his next move. In the middle of accelerating, he applied the brakes and counter-steered the bike to the exit ramp. I got scrunched up onto my drivers back. It was a short exit, so he braked hard. We rolled to a gas station at the exit. My driver kept our helmets on and we waited for a few minutes. We decided that place would be a good place to top-off with fuel and to grab an early morning snack. When we finally returned to the interstate, we were scanning vehicles for that gray pickup truck, but never saw it again.

We reached Texarkana, but the dealership was closed. Rather than waiting 30 minutes until they opened, we hit the road.

Before noon, the ambient air thermometer on the handlebar fluctuated between 105 to over 110 – while we were rolling. We stopped about every 45 minutes and we drank lots of water. We stopped at the Harley-Davidson dealership in Waco. Those guys were biker doggie friendly and they let me stay there for an hour to get out of the heat. John, a manager, printed route instructions around Austin to help us avoid traffic and to keep us rolling. It was very helpful, but we got stuck in the Austin traffic anyway. A radio station reported it was 104 IN THE SHADE!

While stuck in traffic, my driver shut off the bike with hopes it would not overheat. Then, he stopped sweating. His arms started looking dry and white. With his Army training, my driver knew he was in trouble. We pulled over to the shoulder of the interstate.

43

My driver filled my bowl with water. While I drank, he pulled out a bottle of water and drank it quickly. One of the cagers rolled down a window and asked if we were OK. My driver said we were trying to stay hydrated. My driver drank a second bottle of water. He kept water in my bowl until I didn't want to drink anymore.

My driver told me lots of times that my slobber on the back of his neck felt really good in the dry heat, so I kept the slobber going. My driver had a 90-minute business teleconference with Tokyo in the late afternoon. We pulled into a truck stop, refueled, bought a bag of ice and lots of bottles of water, and sat in the shade with a hot, dry breeze for two hours. The bike was in the shade, and the thermometer read about 105. I lay on the ground with my back against the bag of ice. Sometimes, I straddled the bag of ice to cool my chest and belly. I snoozed while my driver was on the phone. The ice felt good! After the phone call, he kept drinking water. He said we weren't rolling until we both peed clear.

We reached our hotel in San Antonio at about sunset. My driver thanked the Lord for watching over us. He ordered a pizza and naked buffalo wings. Mmmmm. That was a good desert after my dinner! We went for a stroll in a grassy area so I could relieve myself. While I was sniffing around, my driver and my mom talked on the phone.

The next morning, the temperature and humidity was very comfortable. South of San Antonio, my driver played with the camera and took some pictures of us while we were riding. There were hardly any cars on the road. We stopped in a rest area, and we saw a sign "Watch out for Snakes"! When we stop in rest areas, my job is to watch the bike. I sometimes bark for my driver to let him know that all is well, and to hurry back!

We visited my driver's parents in Beeville for a few hours. I went to the doggie hotel in Odem to spend the weekend and play with new friends in an outdoor play area. My doggie hotel was pawesome! My room was air conditioned. It had a comfortable bed, but I preferred the stone tile floor. It also had a doggie door so I could go outside when it was cool in the morning and evening, then go inside when it was hot during the day. My driver rode to Kingsville for his reunion. He was gone for two nights. I admit that I wondered if he was coming back for me. I know he loves me, so there must be a good reason I couldn't be with him. He promised that he would be back in two days and we would ride more.

Playing with the camera

My driver arrived a few hours after sunrise two days later – just like he promised. I was tired and hot from playing, but I was ready to roll. A cool front passed through Texas, and the temperatures were much cooler with lower humidity. The road to Houston (US-77 and US-59) had light traffic and it was a nice, leisurely ride. Houston to Beaumont, however, had heavy traffic. We were grateful to the Lord for the cooler temperatures.

We reached Baton Rouge, Louisiana and stayed at a really nice hotel, one of the few that we could find that would accept me. We asked the hotel manager about dog friendly restaurants. The only one she identified was a Hooters. So, we went to Hooters. They let me eat outside with my driver and the ladies gave me ice water. The staff and customers were very friendly. I ate a whole Texas Steak Sammich and fries, then had my regular MRE dinner at the hotel. Mmmmmm! Woooof! That was good!

***Steak   sammich   dinner   in   Baton   Rouge,
Louisiana***

After we ate, we sat outside for a bit. A man, a woman and two children came to us. They asked my driver if I ride on the Harley. The man and my driver talked while his wife and two children pet me.

"Where are you from?" asked the man.

"Kipling, North Carolina," replied my driver. My driver explained the location in relation to Raleigh.

"Where y'all headed?" asked the man.

My driver told him about our destination being Kingsville, Texas, but we are returning home. The man was curious about our route, so my driver explained our route to Kingsville and our route home.

"You must be rich," stated the man.

"Why do you think that?" asked my driver.

"You ain't got a watch and you're travelling with a dog on a motorcycle," replied the man.

My driver replied "Rich in money? No. If I consider the blessings of God, then most certainly."

"Blessings like in being rich?" asked the man.

My driver replied, "Blessings like the gift Jesus gave us so that we could go to Heaven. Blessings can come in many forms. For example, having good weather, the bike running well, finding a hotel and restaurant that will accept Chewy, meeting people along the way. I think meeting you and your family is a blessing to Chewy and me."

"Whatever it is you have, I'd like some of it," stated the woman.

My driver suggested they pray to find a Bible-based church and meet others who share the same belief in God and His Son. I let the kids keep petting and massaging me while the man and woman talked with my driver.

When we returned to our hotel room, my driver felt different. We prayed together, and my driver talked with me. He told me that he feels blessed, but God might let satan test us. Little did we know that two months after we returned home, my driver and I would be hit and my driver would be injured. About eight months after we were hit, my driver would lose his job and be unemployed for three years. I'll bark about that in another chapter. My driver was worried and he did his best to stay away from depression, but he kept his faith that God had a reason.

The next day, we rolled east on the road that travels north of New Orleans. We rolled northeast into Mississippi. The temperature and humidity continued to be comfortable. We stopped at the Harley-Davidson dealership in Meridian and learned that there are only four H-D dealerships in Mississippi. That explains why we could not find one in Hattiesburg. The dealership in Meridian was biker doggie friendly.

After a brief stop in Meridian, we rode to a huge Harley-Davidson dealership in Birmingham, Alabama. Those guys are friendly. There were several members of their H.O.G. chapter in the shop. They invited us to ride with them on any weekend. We learned that this dealership is the second largest in the US.

The scenery between Birmingham and Chattanooga was beautiful. I tilted my head left and right when my driver said "Chattanooga". To me, that's an interesting hooman word. "Chattanooga!" We arrived in Chattanooga about an hour before sunset.

Before leaving Chattanooga the next morning, I met a new friend. I think he was a Pekinese or something like that. I let him sit on my driver's seat for a photo. We rode north, then merged onto I-40 eastbound, enjoyed the scenic ride and stopped a few times along the way.

Meeting a new friend in Chattanooga

We stopped at a rest area east of Swannanoa and ran into a Harley-Davidson employee from Milwaukee. He was in a car, which we assume was a rental car. We can't remember his name, but he had a Harley-Davidson University short-sleeved shirt with "Faculty" on the front left of his shirt. He was visiting dealerships in the Carolinas and was heading to Birmingham to visit the dealership. The H-D man took lots of pictures of me, and my driver got a picture of him with me. I think every person associated with Harley-Davidson are friendly.

We arrived home before sunset on Tuesday. I had no idea when we left seven days earlier that I would be riding 3,436 miles. My driver told me he hoped to be able to take a longer trip and ride to a place called California, or, at least, Arizona.

My ride to Texas was a pawesome adventure and a learning expawrience.

Tongue in the Wind

Chapter 10: Behind Barz

I started writing for Behind Barz Motorcycle Magazine a couple of years after I started riding. It all started when I barktated stories to my driver to submit for H.O.G. Wash, the newsletter for Raleigh H.O.G. My first long article was about taking my driver to Texas. I barktated the story and helped my driver shrink it to about 700 words. Hoomans seemed to like the article.

I was riding for less than three years, and it was after Christmas. My driver and I received an email from Debbie "Doobie" Sykes, the founding Editor-in-Chief of Behind Barz Motorcycle Magazine. I think Doobie and I met at the Miracle League Ride a few months earlier, and Doobie put a picture of me in her magazine. It was in the issue that was released the month of Thanksgiving.

In the email, Doobie invited me to attend one of their Bike Nite events as a celebrity guest. Me? A celebrity? No way! We were just a dog and his driver who both have a love for riding and trying to follow God's guidance the best we can.

A couple of months later, we attended a Behind Barz event in Wilson, North Carolina. It was pawesome! I was allowed to sit in a race car and meet the driver, Crow Whitley! Crow is pawesome!

At the event, my driver and I met Doobie. I'm not sure how the conversation started, but the outcome was an invitation to submit an article and two or three pictures. Behind Barz is a full color, glossy magazine. It's perfect for photographs where a picture can "say" things that is difficult to bark into hooman words. Well, I barktated an article to my driver, my driver submitted it, and the rest is history.

After that specific issue was published, Doobie contacted my driver and invited us to continue submitting articles. The timing was pawfect because I had adventures to barktate.

It didn't take long for me to regularly barktate my adventures. Contrary to what hoomans believe, we did not receive any pay, compensation or money. We never asked to be paid. I was like a guest repawter, and Doobie usually allocated three pages for my articles and pictures. Most of my articles were about events we attended. Many of my articles were connected directly and indirectly with the military and non-profit organizations.

Behind Barz Motorcycle Magazine, Sept-Oct 2015 Issue

Doobie had rights to edit our stories, but she rarely did. Occasionally, we noticed where she added a couple of sentences to clarify something, which we appreciated. After all, I'm just a dog who doesn't bark hooman, and my driver is just a hooman.

Barktating stories for Doobie's magazine was a blessing. It allowed my driver and me to have a collection of stories for my pawtobiography. As my driver and I attended events, many hoomans who I never met asked my driver if I was Chewy. They pet me and many told me they enjoyed my stories. Some called me the word "faymoose" and some called me a "legend". We will always be just a dog and his driver trying to serve the Lord while honoring our military, helping non-profit organizations, and putting smiles on faces along the way.

Tongue in the Wind

Chapter 11: Biker Dog Down

A couple of weeks after we celebrated my seventh birthday. My driver said that I needed groceries, so we mounted up to ride to Apex.

Before I continue explaining, let me take a minute to bark a term. A "cage" is a car. Bikers call them cages because of the metal shell that protects the hoomans inside. A cager is a person who drives a cage. If a biker is driving a cage, that pawson is a cager, too. Cage or cager is NOT a derogatory term.

We stopped on the road behind a cage. We were about one car length behind the cage and we lined up behind the cage's driver. The cager was doing something in the cage because we could see her moving around and reaching to the backseat. I looked over my driver's shoulder to see why we weren't rolling. We were patient and waited about a minute.

My driver saw the back-up lights turn on. He put his thumb on the horn button. The cager started backing up towards us. My bike's horn blasted. The cager kept coming and her rear driver side hit our front right. The bike fell hard to the left and shot my driver out of the saddle. He landed on his head in the oncoming traffic lane. My saddle held me until the bike came to a rest on its side. I slid out of the saddle and stood on my paws.

I stood on the hot pavement and looked at my driver. My harness was snap-linked to the saddle, so I couldn't go anywhere. The bike shut off, but the CD player was still running. My driver was face down about eight feet from the bike. He was parallel to the bike with his feet facing the direction of the front tire and his head facing the direction of the rear tire. His face was pointing towards the bike, but I couldn't see his eyes because of his riding glasses. He wasn't moving.

Hoomans quickly went to him. I think my driver was talking with someone because another person knew to go to the right saddlebag to fetch my leash.

After several minutes, a white, box-shaped, diesel truck showed up with flashing lights. By then, I was moved away from the bike. I watched pawple work on my driver. He wasn't moving. They put him on a bed-like thing and put him in the truck. The truck sat in the street for a long time. They were waiting for someone to provide "clearance" to give them permission to take my driver to a big hospital with a spine trauma unit.

My mom showed up. I was excited to see her. Then, Keith and his wife, Christine, showed up. The plan was for Keith and Christine to take me home, while my mom went to the hospital. I couldn't understand why I couldn't go with my driver. Before my my departed, Keith and Christine told her that she was going to be a grandma again!

At home, I waited and waited and waited. It had been dark outside for many hours by the time I heard my mom's car in the driveway. My driver was with her. I was excited to see them, but I was careful around my driver. My driver was loopy. Very loopy. I mean, VERY loopy!

He had no visible injuries and no broken bones. The helmet probably saved his life, but landing on his head hurt his neck and upper back. When he stumbled slowly into the house, he didn't seem to be feeling anything. My mom helped my driver to bed, and he stayed there for a loooong time. I laid at the foot of the bed. Whenever he moved, I sat up to check on him. I only left him for dinner and to go outside to pee or poop.

A couple of weeks passed. My driver went to Ray Price Harley-Davidson to sign documents that gave them permission to repair my bike. A friend saw my driver and told him that she was sorry to hear about Chewy. Another friend went to my driver and said the same thing. Another told him that he heard that Chewy was killed in the accident.

It appears that soon after the crash, one person (let's say, Person N from the northern USA) asked another (let's say Person S from the southern USA) if we were OK. I'm guessing that conversation went something like this.

Person S: Did you hear that Chewy and his driver were hit?
Person N: Were they hurt?
Person S: "Chewy's day-yed"
Now, Person S was saying "Chewy's dad", but with the southern accent, it was probably translated as "Chewy's dead". I

think maybe that's how the rumor got started that I was killed. If it's not true, it's a cute story!

My mom and my driver engaged Gary Poole in Chapel Hill to help us recover expenses from the crash. The driver of the cage didn't have enough insurance coverage. Fortunately, a couple of years before the crash, Stan Simmerson encouraged Raleigh H.O.G. members to look into uninsured/underinsured coverage. Stan is a medical professional at Duke Hospital. At the meeting, he explained that one day in ICU or emergency room could cost about $30,000. If a cager had the minimum insurance coverages, only two to three days of hospital care would be covered. Gary was a guest speaker at the meeting that evening. A few days after that H.O.G. meeting, my mom and my driver contacted our insurance carrier. For a few dollars a month, they added uninsured/underinsured coverage.

My driver tried to keep working, but he was in constant pain. Months later, he eventually lost his job after a new boss started in the company. My driver understood that he was no longer doing well at this job, and that his new boss needed someone who could perform. The company helped my driver because of what he did to help the company.

The first attorney that my pawrents engaged happened to be the first one who sent someone to our house to talk with us. The person who met with us rode a bike, so he seemed to understand. That's where the connection seemed to end. It seemed like nothing was happening. My driver remembered Gary and several Raleigh H.O.G. members recommended him, so we engaged him. It was a pawtastic decision!

We recovered our medical expenses, but it took over four years. Although my driver was unemployed for a long time, he did not receive lost wages. My pawrents dipped into their retirement fund. My driver said he probably would not be able to retire. But, he also said that retirement is not in the Bible, so maybe he's not meant to retire since he is one of God's followers. Moses, Abraham, Israel, Isaiah and many more followers of God continued doing what they did until God called them to Heaven. Whether or not my driver is able to retire will be God's will, not my driver's will.

It was financially difficult, but my driver and my mom saw blessings. If my driver was still working, we would not have had time to attend many funerals of Fallen Heroes and Passing Veterans. We attended a lot of events, too. A few people knew that my driver was unemployed. Some of the simple gestures were such a blessing to us. For example, we rode to a gas station near Raleigh/Durham International Airport to stage with the Patriot Guard and escort a Fallen Hero to a funeral home. As we stopped at a gas pump and my driver dismounted, Ol' Bill (aka "Jammer", aka "OB1") swiped his credit card at the pump and handed the hose to my driver as he turned around. That touched my driver and me. A few others anonymously blessed us. When my driver and I went to Ray Price H-D for an oil change, someone paid for the oil change while we were waiting. My driver set aside money to pay for it, but the blessing of that anonymous person allowed us to have gas money to attend funerals that we otherwise would have had to pass up. To those anonymous hoomans, my driver and I bark a sincere thank you.

We had a number of close calls over the years. One time, we attended the funeral of a homeless veteran with the Patriot Guard. It was cold and during the month of Christmas. We were nearly taken out by a deer and a cager within minutes of each other.

The night before our trip from Kipling (our home township) to Charlotte, my driver's church said a prayer for travelling mercies for us at their weekly Prayer Group meeting. We left the house at o'dark thirty (in military language, my driver says that means very early in the morning while it is still dark).

It was still dark when we were southbound on US 15/501 east of Carthage. We had been on the road about 30-45 minutes. I started moving around in my seat, and that was causing our Harley to wiggle on the highway. After a few seconds, my driver turned his head to the right to tell me to sit, and then he saw it: a deer charging toward us. The deer was at about forty-five degrees to our right and about five feet from us. My driver opened the throttle. He was so close that we saw the deer's eyes, nose, and antlers. We know it wasn't Rudolf because his nose was black. It happened too fast to count the number of points on his rack. We shot in front of the deer and the deer crossed the road behind us. If we had braked or slowed down, the deer could have T-boned us. I squirmed around in my seat to look back and watched the deer run off into the dark. How did my driver know to accelerate and not brake? We think God was watching over us, but wanted us to stay alert.

A few minutes later, my driver and I saw the side profile of a car coming towards the highway. It was still dark, so what we saw was the car's left side headlight beam and a side marker light. It looked like the car was slowing down a little. My driver tapped the front brake to disengage the cruise control. As we came to the intersection, the car ran the stop sign and made a right turn in front of us. My driver counter-steered and threw the bike into the oncoming traffic lane. He threw the bike so hard to the left that we still don't know how he was able to maintain control of the bike without running off the road or laying the bike down. We cleared the left side of the car by less than two feet when we shot past the car. We moved back into the southbound lane and my driver slowed down and goosed the throttle between gears. I was ready to give that cager the paw and a good grrrrowl. My driver watched the car's headlights in the rear view mirror as we slowed down. The cager kept his distance and then did a U-turn. We pulled into a gas station in Carthage so I could check my seat and my driver could check his underwear.

At this point, I had less than four years in the saddle (or less than 28 doggie years). My driver had over 35 years in the saddle. Maneuvering around that car at highway speed was more than just experience – God was watching over us and reminding us that He has His hand of protection on us. As one of my social media friends posted, "Jesus took the handlebars." I'm sure counter-steering was a small part of it. It's one thing to know how to counter-steer, but it's another to make counter-steering part of normal riding so that it becomes a reflex reaction. My driver nearly always counter-steers. Those who ride with my driver and me oftentimes see my driver with one hand using a camera, and the other hand on the throttle. My driver uses counter-steering to maintain control of the bike in turns while using the camera. Since counter-steering is part of his normal riding, when he needs to react in a split second, his normal reaction is to counter-steer. I just know that when he counter-steers as a reaction, he doesn't have time to warn me and I get bounced around in my saddle!

Chapter 12: Chewy Cam

Tree. Tree. Tree. Car. Tree. Tree. Fire Hydrant. Whoa! Stop! That's what I see when I ride with my driver on our Harley-Davidson.

My driver was curious about what I look at when we ride. He cannot see me, unless he adjusts the mirrors. But, if he adjusts the mirrors to see me, he cannot see beside and behind the bike.

Sometimes, I may see something and I will shift around a bit to get into a better position to look at that something. I may sit higher and rest my chin on my driver's shoulder, look around my driver's arm, or sometimes look at bikers beside us or behind us.

I have a battery operated, mini video camera that attaches to the front of my helmet with velcro. We call that camera the "Chewy Cam". The first time we used the Chewy Cam was escorting the remains of a passing veteran from Charlotte to Salisbury National Cemetery.

After we returned home, my driver processed the video files and watched them. He noticed that I tended to look back towards riders, and look at various items along the side of the interstate. As we rolled through Salisbury on the video, my driver noticed something – I would spot a fire hydrant ahead of us, track it as we passed it, then look at it briefly behind us. He counted me tracking over 30 fire hydrants! He also noticed that I watched and tracked a dumpster and a port-o-john. Now, my driver knows a little bit of what I look at while riding. Pawesome!

There was a funeral mission in northeast North Carolina for Sergeant Willie McLawhorn, US Army, KIA 12 December 2010, Afghanistan. It was a cold day. I think the temperatures were single digit when we left our house at o'dark thirty.

While returning home, we were southbound on I-95 rolling towards Smithfield and Benson. We are accustomed to cages passing us on the interstate, slowing down, and then rolling next to us while they check me out.

Weeks after the funeral, someone sent us a link to a video posted on a popular video website. My driver noticed the date of the post and what I was wearing. He found the video of the

Sergeant McLawhorn mission. We searched my Chewy Cam video for things that appeared on the posted video. It took a while, but we found the car from which the video of me was taken. My driver snipped out that portion of the video and posted it as a reply to the video of me. It was so cool when the car passengers saw themselves videoing me!

We used the Chewy Cam a few times, but the video and sound quality was not very good. The Chewy Cam was sold by a small company in North Carolina. Sadly, the video camera was not manufactured in the USA, and it didn't last very long. After my driver created a ruckus, the company owners replaced the camera. But, that camera didn't last very long, too.

Chapter 13: Slobber Factor

If you know us dogs, then you know we pant and slobber when it's hot (and sometimes when it's cold, too). Put a dog on a bike, and the slobber floats in the air! Riding on a bike with a fairing and windshield changes the air flow. I can only bark for my Harley-Davidson Electra Glide Ultra Classic.

My driver owned a few bikes over his life time, and each creates a different air flow, depending upon the accessories. For example on the Ultra, the air flows over the top and around the sides of the windshield. In some areas behind my driver, the air flow circles and goes forward, depending upon the speed and head winds. There is also air flow that travels under the fairing and over and up from the gas tank. If you ever see a man with a beard riding a H-D Ultra on the highway, you will notice that his beard floats upward in front of his face, rather than flow around his neck.

At about 30-45 mph and less, my slobber drips onto the top of the saddlebag lid. A lot of the slobber gets carried back and it falls on the top of the tour pack (trunk). My driver puts a coat of wax on those areas often because my slobber leaves spots on the paint that are hard to buff out.

At about 45-55 mph, the air flow will float some of my slobber forward and it lands on the back of the windshield and slowly drips down the windshield before drying. Most of the slobber lands on my driver's shoulder or the back of his neck and helmet, but some of the slobber reaches the windshield.

At interstate speeds, particularly with a head wind, my slobber drifts forward. The air flow coming from under the fairing is diverted upward by the gas tank, which pushes my slobber upward to the air flow coming over the top of the fairing. Guess where my slobber lands? My slobber splatters onto my driver's glasses. If the air flow is just right, it'll land on his face and sometimes on his lips, especially if I let go of a big, juicy, heavy slobber.

On those hot summer days on the interstate when we exit to refuel, you'll see my driver clean the dried slobber spots from his glasses and my doggles. He rarely complained because it's all part of a dog and a hooman riding together.

I get motion sickness sometimes. I vomited while sailing, while riding in the car, while on the bike on Tail of the Dragon, and even when we were riding in the Raleigh Christmas Parade. My driver cleans the mess, makes sure I'm OK, and we continue.

On one day, we were heading home on US-401. We were south of Garner, North Carolina and heading south on a section that was four lanes with a 45 mph speed limit.

A white car was tailgating us. He was inches from the rear of our bike. My driver hand signaled the cager to try to communicate to the driver to move to the left lane. The cager didn't shift lanes, so my driver signaled and move to the left lane. The cager changed lanes and stayed on our tail. My driver should have asked me to give a paw signal – I would have given him a good one!

The cager was taking pictures. I thought about giving him the paw. That cager should have backed off and let his passenger take pictures. If my driver decelerated, that cage would have rear ended us.

My driver hand signaled the cager to move to the right lane. He didn't, so my driver moved to the right lane. At about that time, I stood up in my seat. My driver got very worried. He had a cager following too close to our tail, and now I'm standing in my seat, which I only do if something is very wrong.

I started acting like I was going to vomit. My driver shifted to the left lane. As he shifted, I vomited into the wind. Since we were riding at about 45 mph, the wind caught the yellowish, slimy goo and blew it onto the hood and windshield of the cage. With the cager still in the right lane, my driver decelerated quickly and the cager passed us. We saw the windshield wipers moving. I wonder how messy that slime became on his windshield.

When we returned home, my driver and I did a high paw before I dismounted and did my post-ride roll in the grass.

I wondered what my slobber would do at 100 mph. Well, I wasn't slobbering at Charlotte Motor Speedway to see where the air flow carried it. I guessed the air flow might push it a little above my driver and maybe it would hang long enough for the rider behind us to get slobbered on. I had the opportunity, but I didn't slobber.

Yes, I rode over 100 mph on Charlotte Motor Speedway, thanks to Evan Parton. My driver commented after our laps that the track looks much larger from the stands than it does when we're driving on the track.

Evan invited me to join the "100 MPH Club" a couple of months before the event. I think I first met Evan at a Patriot Guard mission in which ol' Bill "Jammer" led the PGR and others in escorting the Travelling Vietnam Wall from the Virginia / North Carolina border to Concord, North Carolina. That would have been around early spring about three years after I started riding. On that day, I remember leaving at o'dark thirty in the morning with Thomas "G.E." Sanders to link up with ol' Bill near Mebane, North Carolina. It was a coooooold day!

Anyway ... when Evan first invited us to Charlotte Motor Speedway, we weren't sure if we would be going because Black Friday is the day my driver and my mom celebrate their anniversary. They were married on Black Friday (loooong story), but it's easier for my driver to remember and it's always on a Friday!

My mom told us to go have fun. So, we did!

The event benefitted the Childrens' Speedway Charities. There were 217 bikes at this event. They were staged outside of the track into packs. When we arrived, we were assigned to a pack. Most of the bikes seemed to be GoldWings since this event was sponsored by Chapter L2 (I think) of the GoldWing Road Riders Association. There was a sprinkling of Harley-Davidsons here and there, as well as other brands. Since my driver rode a GoldWing before he adopted me and was a member of GWRRA, he felt comfortable being among them.

About every 30 minutes, a pack would mount up and roll through the tunnel onto the track's infield. While waiting in the pre-staging area, I put the leash on my driver and took him to various packs to meet hoomans. We then heard our pack being called to stand-by, so we returned to our bike. We noticed hoomans putting on helmets and mounting their bikes, so we did the same.

Before this event, Jeff Davis gave us a helmet camera, which we called the "JD" cam. This was a better quality camera than the small micro-camera that attaches to my helmet, which we call the "Chewy Cam". We used both cameras mounted on each of our helmets so that my driver would not have to ride one-handed while holding a hand-held camera. He's accustomed to driving with one hand holding a camera. But, we never took pictures rolling at 100 mph.

My laps on Charlotte Motor Speedway were dedicated to Fallen Heroes and their Gold Star Families. The flags on my Harley-Davidson were the same flags that accompanied me on my first ride across the USA in honor and remembrance of our Fallen Heroes. My driver and I had a moment of silence before rolling to the infield. A few names that came to mind include Michael Rodriguez, Adam Ginett, Mark Adams, Scott Brunkhorst, Lance Eakes, Willie McLawhorn, Michael Spivey, Mikey Swink, James McClamrock, Amy Sinkler, Jeff Sherer, Mark Bradley, Aaron Blasjo, Lucas Elliott, Ross Carver and many, many more. We also said a prayer for Cory Remsburg, an Army Ranger I met the previous year who was wounded in action and overcoming a traumatic brain injury. It's hard to forget the names of those we honored.

It was time! We rolled through the tunnel and onto the infield. It was pawesome riding on the infield! The bikes stayed in line, with about 20 bikes in our pack. Another pack was already in line near the entrance to pit row, and a pack was already on pit row. We kept our helmets on and stayed close to the bike. I stayed in my saddle and chilled.

A safety briefing was given. After the briefing, we stayed near the bikes until it was time to mount up and roll onto pit row.

We lined up in pairs on pit row. One of the guards was helping the officials. When she saw me, she became very excited! I mean, she was so excited that her voice changed to a very happy scream. She petted me and took pictures. My helmet cam captured that meeting. She is a cool lady!

When signaled, we fired up the motor. It wasn't too long before we started accelerating down pit row and merged onto the race track. We were in a hard acceleration. We were in the middle of the track going into turn two, and we could feel the bike slightly accelerate going down the slight grade onto the back straight-away.

By then, my driver was in sixth gear and the throttle was wide open. There were a few bikes ahead of us, but most of our pack was behind us. A pace car stayed in front of the pack.

On the back straight-away, it was very windy sitting behind my driver. I tucked in behind him to use him as a wind shield, like I sometimes do when we're on the interstate. I've been in windy conditions riding on an interstate with a strong head wind, but I have never been this fast on pavement. The wind pushed my helmet so that it tilted back on my head. That made the Chewy Cam point slightly upwards. The track surface was smooth and the bike wasn't vibrating as much as I thought it would.

As we came out of turn four, we were among the lead in the pack. My driver wasn't sure what line to take going into the slight dog leg on the front straight-away. "Dog" leg? That's an odd name for that bend in the road. My driver gauged the line by watching the pace car.

We went high into turn one. That was intentional. As we came out of turn two, we had a slightly steeper downhill grade going into the back straight-away. With our two cylinder motor, that gave us a little bit of a push. My driver looked at the speedometer on the back stretch long enough to see that we were over 100 mph. He said he didn't look at the speedometer again because he was focused on the track and the bikes.

On the back straight-away, a yellow GoldWing passed us on the right. He was probably rolling over 120 mph with his six cylinders. Those GoldWings moved faster on the track, but, in my opawnion, the Harley-Davidsons SOUNDED totally pawesome with their throttles wide open! Regardless, I became a member of the "100 MPH Club" on that day.

Charlotte Motor Speedway after riding over 100 mph, Photo by Evan Parton

Chapter 14: Charlie Mike

Charlie Mike is military phonetics for the letters C and M. Charlie Mike also means continue the mission.

The Combat Veterans Motorcycle Association (CVMA) Chapter NC 15-1 held an Iron Butt ride when I was about eight years old in mid-summer. The ride was an Iron Butt Saddle Sore 1000, meaning we were riding 1,000 miles in 24 hours. This ride was in honor and remembrance of Prisoners of War and those Missing in Action (POW/MIA) during the Vietnam War.

My driver and I didn't know anyone on this ride. This ride had special meaning to us because of my mom's uncle, Alvah Denton. You see, Uncle Alvah was in the Army Air Corps during World War II. His aircraft went down over water. Alvah's remains and the aircraft were never found. My mom's grandmother was a Gold Star Mother, but probably did not know what that represents. President Roosevelt signed a letter sent to my mom's grandmother. My mom's dad, Toot Denton (Alvah's younger brother), was given the letter when his mom passed. When my mom's parents passed, they left the letter for her. That letter carries a special meaning with my pawrents because of what they do to honor and remember our Fallen through the Patriot Guard, the Flags for Fallen Military, and more organizations.

It was hot and humid. This ride was recognized by the Iron Butt Association, but all of the riders rode for the mission, not the patch. This Iron Butt ride was unique because (1) the entire route was within North Carolina, and (2) we travelled country roads, highways (2 and 4 lanes), and interstates. Kevin "Cowboy" Desmond from a Christian Motorcyclists Association chapter volunteered to follow in his truck pulling a 17' trailer containing a fully-equipped mobile motorcycle repair shop. Cowboy is a very special person!

I knew something was going to happen when I watched my driver put two cans of food and lots of treats into a saddlebag. Before we left the house, my driver poured anti-Monkey Butt powder in his pants. He put some in my seat. I appreciated the thought until we got on the highway headed to Lillington. At highway speed, the butt powder was floating out of my seat. Because of the air flow behind the fairing, we had a cloud of butt powder circulating around us. From behind, we must have looked like we were smokin'. I sneezed and sneezed and sneezed. Let's not do that again!

Before going to the staging area at the Veterans Memorial Park in Lillington, my driver stopped at a gas station to fill-up. When he hit the starter button, we heard the starter clunk and we lost all electrical power. My driver thought we blew the relay or a fuse.

I sniff checked the bike and told my driver it was the butt powder's fault. He called my mom, who was on her way to the Veterans Memorial Park. When she arrived at the gas station, my driver and I were trying to figure out the problem. My driver asked my mom to go to the staging area and tell the ride leader (Charles "StrangeMan" Lyles) that we broke down. I decided to go with my mom to supawvise.

While we were gone, my driver called Randy at Ray Price H-D. Randy talked my driver through possible things to check before calling for a tow. My mom found a Harley mechanic and we brought him to my driver. Michael "Glock" Mills is a CVMA member going on the Memorial Ride, and he's a Harley-Davidson mechanic.

When we arrived at the gas station, my driver was putting the saddle back on my bike. He found the problem. The battery terminal bolts were a half turn from being tight, but it seemed to be enough to cause the problem. My saddle takes time to put on my bike, so Glock installed the side panels and saddlebags while my driver mounted my saddle.

The ride departed shortly after noon on Friday. It was hot! We had 17 hoomans on 14 bikes, plus me. We ran into traffic in Fayetteville, and it felt hotter while idling. Once south of Fayetteville, the temperature was bearable as long as we were rolling. We rode south toward Rockingham, then west on US-74 towards Charlotte. We reached Charlotte during Friday afternoon rush hour on US-74. It was hot again, and there were lots of traffic lights.

Westbound on US-74

A VFW post in Charlotte had pizza waiting for us, so we inhaled a quick dinner. I shared my pizza with my driver. We lost a lot of time in traffic in Fayetteville and Charlotte. After we left the VFW post, the group was split due to traffic. The lead group stopped at a gas station, while someone rode to find the other group. I think we were at that gas station for over an hour, which was more time clicking off the clock. No one thought of going ahead with the ride because we wanted to remain together as one unit. Once the two groups rejoined, we were rolling again.

Waiting with Brian Volk in Charlotte, North Carolina

We rode into a beautiful sunset as we rode toward Asheville! We rode on a bridge and there was fog coming from a deep gorge. The fog swirled with the air flow of the bikes. It was a pawesome sight!

We stopped for fuel and changed to night glasses; I put on my clear lens Sopwith Camel pilot-looking goggles.

Getting to know Dagger and Wizard at a fuel stop near Asheville, North Carolina

We reached the halfway mark near Burlington a little after midnight. About three hours later, we arrived at a VFW post in Roanoke Rapids for rehydration, coffee, stretching and snacks. StrangeMan gave a refresher safety briefing. He noticed we were riding closer to each other in the night. He encouraged us to increase the gap between the bikes. With the critters near the road, we were putting ourselves at risk if a critter wandered onto the road. To sort of quote StrangeMan as he ended his safety briefing, this ride "separates the men from the boys, the women from the girls, and the dogs from the puppies!" I think they were already recognizing that underneath my soft fur was a tough dog who didn't complain about anything.

We rolled into the sunrise between Greenville and Jacksonville. In Jacksonville, we stopped at the Vietnam Veterans Memorial where other CVMA and Rolling Thunder members were waiting for us with refreshments. We picked up a couple of riders to go with us for the remainder of the ride. We stopped at the USS North Carolina battleship in Wilmington, where more hoomans met us with refreshments and we picked up more riders.

When we rolled from Battleship Park, we rode on I-40 west toward Benson and Dunn. It wasn't long before the traffic on the interstate came to a halt. There may have been a wreck ahead of us. After several minutes of not moving, the group rolled onto the shoulder and rode slowly on the shoulder to the next exit. From there, we rode south to US-421, then rolled west toward Dunn.

We reached our 1,000-mile mark a little after noon. We had been on the road for about 23.5 hours. We were about 15 miles east of Dunn at the time. We accomplished the mission, but we wanted to arrive in Dunn on time, too. We stopped at a gas station, and StrangeMan made it clear that we were to take on fuel and go. We were not to dismount! There was some celebrating and thumbs up from the saddles. My driver fueled the bike and we pulled away from the gas pump to line up with other bikes that had already refueled. Bikers were giving me a thumbs up, and some were barking. Before we rolled, Dagger and StrangeMan pointed to me and one of them yelled "IronMutt!" That's how I earned my road name! It's such a pawesome road name because it fits! Above all, it was an honor to be accepted by other bikers who are veterans or still serving.

When we arrived in Dunn, a lot of bikers and cagers met us, along with a fire truck, and police and sheriffs escort. We were escorted from Dunn to Lillington, where we had the closing ceremonies. Hoomans who knew me were surprised that I made it. I walked around and greeted lots of hoomans. They seemed excited to see me, and that made me excited to be there.

We had no accidents and no break downs during the ride! Well, sort of. Cowboy had a trailer tire go down, but he was able to replace the tire and link-up with us.

This was a great ride for a great cause, and all of the riders looked out for each other. Is it possible that I was the first biker dog to complete an iron butt ride? Probably not.

After we returned home, my driver gave me a cool bath in the front yard. He took a shower and we both fell asleep on the living room floor. I didn't move all Saturday night and my mom said that we both snored LOUDLY!

Greeting Angie Norris and many more friends after returning to Lillington

Chapter 15: Ride Across the USA

In observance of Memorial Day, I took my driver and Thomas Sanders across the USA in honor and remembrance of Fallen Soldiers, Sailors, Airmen and Marines. The bikers we ride with call them "Fallen Heroes". I was about nine years old for this ride.

It was a pawtastic expawrience! We ran into 50 mph headwinds in the Texas Panhandle and into New Mexico, 110° temperatures in Arizona, drizzle crossing the Golden Gate Bridge in San Francisco, snow showers east of Sacramento, 40-50 mph crosswinds in northeast Colorado and into Nebraska, and we saw the fog roll into Chicago from Lake Michigan. I sniffed the breeze off the Atlantic coast, Gulf of Mexico, Pacific coast, and Lake Michigan. We handed out over 700 of my cards, and found only three hoomans who knew about Gold Star and Blue Star Mothers. For those who don't know, a Blue Star Mother is a mother who has a child who has served or who is currently serving in our military. A Gold Star Mother is a mother who lost a child while in service to our country.

Planning began earlier in the year. My driver prays frequently and asked for guidance and wisdom, particularly since he was still unemployed. During one of his prayers, a feeling came over him to see and expawrience the land that God created. My driver knows that Jesus sacrificed his human life for our eternal salvation. My driver also knows that our men and women in uniform are willing to sacrifice their lives for our protection and freedom. It's not just our men and women in the military who put their lives on the line, but also our law enforcement officers who put their lives on the line for the freedom and protection of the communities they serve. This road trip would be for them, too. Planning a trip from North Carolina to South Texas would be easy compared to a cross-country ride.

My driver and I made three copies of a Fallen Heroes roster. That roster had the names of those who gave the ultimate sacrifice during the Iraq and Afghanistan wars. Although we carried that roster, our mission was in honor and remembrance of ALL Fallen Heroes. Our roster had 5,998 heroes – sons and daughters, husbands and wives, fathers and mothers, brothers and sisters, aunts and uncles. We also carried a folded US flag, Christian flag, Honor and Remember flag, and a Patriot Guard Riders flag.

Fallen Heroes Rosters

On the first day of our mission, Chuck Ballas joined us near Warsaw, North Carolina and rode with us to Oak Island, then Elizabethtown. At Oak Island, Brunswick Air flew us along a section of the Atlantic coast in a Cessna 172. Thomas sat in the pilot's seat. I think he had the controls for part of the flight. That was my first time in a plane!

The next day, we stayed at home so we could attend the send-off and return of the Triangle Flight of Honor at Raleigh/Durham airport. Flight of Honor is a non-profit organization which flies WWII veterans to Washington, DC to visit the WWII Memorial. During the event, I met Blue Star Moms, USO volunteers, and lots of World War II veterans. Renee Adams, the Gold Star Mother of Mark Adams, Sergeant, US Marine Corps, KIA 15 October 2005, Iraq, escorted my driver and me to the gate.

We had special permission to go through the airport security checkpoint. That was a first for me. I had to take off my collar because of the metal. I had to make sure I stayed connected with my driver, so I made sure his hand was on the scruff of my neck.

He didn't need to grab me. He just guided me as the security officer gave us instructions. At the gate, I greeted the veterans as they entered the terminal. After the veterans deboarded the plane, my driver and I walked back with them. I rode an escalator and a moving sidewalk. I rode an escalator before, but I didn't know what to think about being on the moving sidewalk and moving without walking. I reckon it's OK for a hooman. If I saw a fire hydrant, how would I stop to sniff and check pee-mail?

On day three, we started our westward trek by going to Maggie Valley, North Carolina, with a stop at Salisbury National Cemetery to honor our Fallen Heroes resting there. We linked up with Richard Chowning west of Albemarle, and he rode with us to Salisbury.

At Salisbury National Cemetery, we visited my friend, Lyle Davenport. He was killed while on his Harley-Davidson. He was a big, gentle man, and like many bikers, he had a compassionate heart and helped many hoomans.

Visiting Lyle at Salisbury National Cemetery

Thomas had a pair of riding gloves that belonged to Kathy Whipkey. I think she left them in Thomas' Gold Wing after a mission. Kathy and Thomas had not yet been to a mission since that day so she could retrieve them. On the ride to Maggie Valley, Thomas had an idea. He told my driver over the CB radio that he was going to take pictures of the gloves at various stops. He called them the "riderless gloves" and it was like a tribute to those who are no longer with us. My driver and I thought it was a pawtastic idea! Thomas returned the gloves to Kathy after they travelled with us across the USAIn Maggie Valley, we stayed at my favorite hotel: Smoky Mountain Lodge. After unpacking, Thomas, my driver and I went to Smackers, where I had chewytizers, a Chewyburger (that's the name Smackers gave the burger), and ice cream. A quiet, clean, comfortable room and a delicious supper – a great combination at the end of a day's ride!

My favorite hotel

The next morning, we rode towards Tail of the Dragon. It was a chilly morning for late spring. Maybe the mountains and elevation made it cooler. Our ride out of Maggie Valley was uphill. A few dozen curves and sweeps later, we were in Cherokee. We rode a four-lane road for awhile, then took a right onto a two-lane road. The road to Tail of the Dragon was just as fun. This would be my second time riding the Tail, so I reckon I could be called a veteran. On US-129 (Tail of the Dragon) we stopped at an overlook. My driver and Thomas chatted about stopping for a few minutes. Well, with the bike traffic stopping and bikers seeing me, the few minutes turned into an hour.

Deals Gap, one end of Tail of the Dragon

After we exited Tail of the Dragon, we rode to Chattanooga, south to Atlanta, then southwest to Columbus, Georgia. We spent the night with my hooman grandma (Aiko) and my hooman uncle (Jim). My furry cousin, Bella, was also a biker dog. Jim was her driver.

The next day, Bella and Jim joined Thomas, my driver and me and we rode to Fort Mitchell National Cemetery in Alabama, then to Dothan. In Dothan, we stopped for lunch. When my driver was in the Army, he served a couple of years at Ft Rucker, which is about 45 minutes from Dothan. He was in a familiar area.

After lunch, my furry cousin and her driver returned to Columbus, while Thomas, my driver and I headed south to Destin, Florida. I'm the honorary mascot of the MeanStreet Riders, a southern rock band whose music is about riding. We planned to link-up with them at their photo shoot near Destin.

About a year before this trip, my driver and I made a montage video and searched for music to use legally. We came across a song called "High on the Hog" by the MeanStreet Riders. My driver contacted their publicist, MeanStreet Mary. The Riders gave us permission to use their song! That was soooo pawesome! Anyway, the Riders go to Maggie Valley often, and we arranged to meet them while they were visiting Maggie Valley. It was a pawesome trip! I met and sniffed members of the band and family: Shannon and his wife, Christine, Dowlin, and Denese (also known as MeanStreet Mary). We visited the Wheels Through Time Museum, and one of the owners rode with the Riders and us on a 1938 Harley-Davidson! The MeanStreet Riders are totally cool and we relate to their music.

Visiting Ft Mitchell National Cemetery, Alabama

Thomas documenting the journey of the riderless gloves at the Florida-Alabama border

So, let's get back to our cross country adventure. MeanStreet Mary, members of the Band, and their friends had a photo shoot. Thomas and I were in their photo shoot, too. We were background pawple for the photos. After the photo shoot, we ate at a Whataburger (my driver's favorite burger place) and spent the night in Destin.

The next day was a long day. We visited the USS Alabama and Battleship Park in Mobile. They have a cool memorial dedicated to the dogs who served in our military. After a short visit in Mobile, we rolled east towards Baton Rouge. It was warm and humid and Thomas learned that I love soft serve ice cream, even though it gave me gas.

Thomas found a barbecue restaurant on his GPS in a town north of New Orleans. We followed the GPS directions. It took us around the same block three times – and we couldn't find the address or the restaurant. We gave up and found a fast food place.

On the interstate between Baton Rouge and Lafeyette, a cager was following us. At one point, they were driving beside us and dropped back. When we exited for fuel, they followed. They were interested in me and thought I was the coolest dog in the world. Thomas explained our ride to them. They thought I was even cooler. The cager asked if she could take a picture. My driver replied, "It'll cost you."

She asked "How much?"

My driver replied "Say prayers for our men and women in uniform."

She said that she already prays for them. My driver thanked her for praying for our service members. I posed proudly for her.

We arrived in Marshall, Texas around midnight. We stayed with Thomas' family. We spent the next day in Marshall. The newspaper in Longview wanted to write a story and take pictures of us. We met them at the Honda motorcycle dealership. Since the Carthage and Marshall area is Thomas' hometown, we gladly let Thomas talk about our adventure. We then went for a short ride on the interstate so the photographer could take some action photos.

The next day, we continued our westward trek. While driving across Texas, we stopped at Strokers in Dallas, based on MeanStreet Mary's recommendation. Our original plan was to stop, walk around a bit, then ride on. While there, we decided to have barbecue brisket for lunch. Strokers was worth the stop! After being in photographs with other pawple visiting Strokers, we mounted up and rolled.

Between Dallas and Amarillo, there wasn't much to see, except the occasional oil cricket – and places to have ice cream to cool down! We spent the night in Amarillo. We stood in the doorway and watched a thunderstorm roll through. It doesn't take much to entertain us.

Since Thomas was plugged into the world on his GoldWing, Ol' Bill "Jammer" sent him a message about a memorial in Irvine, California. Thomas, my driver, and I discussed making the memorial our west coast destination. That sounded good to me! The question, though, was whether or not we would be able to find it.

Before leaving Amarillo, we topped off our fuel tanks. Thomas also filled a two-gallon gas can that he carried in the trailer he was pulling. We called his trailer the "Chuck Wagon".

We had strong headwinds from Amarillo to Albuquerque. We estimated the winds at 30 mph. Our low fuel light usually turns on at about 140 miles. Although Thomas carried more fuel, he was pulling the Chuck Wagon and his low fuel light would turn on at about 140 to 150 miles. With the headwinds, our low fuel light went on at 90 miles. My driver thought something was wrong. Thomas and my driver chatted on the CB radio and both had their fuel lights on. We don't remember seeing any gas stations, but we normally didn't start looking until we had about 120 miles on the tank.

We kept rolling into the head wind. We saw a sign indicating an exit ahead with a gas station. My driver radioed Thomas. Before we reached the exit ramp, Thomas radioed that he was out of fuel. I looked back at Thomas as he pulled onto the shoulder. My driver checked the mirrors and saw Thomas on the shoulder. My driver pulled onto the shoulder, shut down the bike, and jogged to Thomas. By the time my driver reached Thomas, he was already pouring fuel into his trike. Thomas asked my driver if he needed fuel. My driver thought we had enough to get to the gas station. My driver came back to the bike, mounted up, fired up the bike and rolled to the exit ramp. As we pulled into the gas station, the bike started sputtering and popping. We were on fumes, but we made it to the gas pump. My bike was probably sputtering from what little fuel was in the fuel line. We pumped 5.1 gallons in our five-gallon tank. Hmmmm. That seemed odd.

Lesson learned: If you come across a gas station in the desert and you're not familiar with the area, gas up whether you need it or not! Unfortunately, we don't remember seeing any open gas stations before this stop.

Crossing the Continental Divide in New Mexico

In Farmington, New Mexico, we checked into the hotel and turned on the TV. We learned that east of Albuquerque, the winds were blowing hard from the west at 50-60 mph. That explained our fuel consumption! My driver went to get some ice from the machine down the hall. I decided to give Thomas some exercise. Thomas opened the door to get something from his bike. When he opened the door, I bolted out of the room. I was looking for my driver. Thomas was chasing me and yelling my name.

My driver returned to the room and didn't see Thomas or me. A few mintues later, Thomas and I came into the room. Thomas was out of breath! I took him for a quarter-mile sprint!

We visited Four Corners, where I put a paw in Arizona, Colorado, New Mexico, and Utah at the same time. It was so pawesome that I could be in four states at one time! We rode north into the southwest corner of Colorado, then west into Utah. We rode through Monument Valley in Utah/Arizona. We stopped somewhere in Monument Valley on the side of the road. Thomas opened up the Chuck Wagon, and we all grabbed drinks and ate leftover pizza. I was very content being on an adventure with my driver and Thomas.

One paw in each of four states: AZ, NM, CO, UT

After lunch, we rode towards a big hole in the ground called a canyon. East of that park, we dismounted and I sniffed around a canyon carved out by the Little Colorado River.

Oak Creek Canyon and Sedona are beautiful! When my driver was in the Army, he was stationed twice in Arizona. The Army designated Arizona as my driver's "regimental home". My driver loves Arizona!

Before continuing our adventure, we had to replace the rear tire. We had a new rear tire installed before leaving North Carolina. This was the first time trying this more expensive brand on our bike. My driver checked our tires and pressure every morning before leaving the hotels. In Amarillo, he was disappointed because he estimated we would need to get a new rear tire in Palm Springs, California. He began lining up the service. By the time we reached Flagstaff, Arizona, he didn't think the rear tire would make it to Palm Springs, so he called dealerships in Arizona. Larry Olsen of Grand Canyon Harley-Davidson in Mayer helped us out. He worked us into a busy schedule for a rear tire and fluid change. We decided to return to Dunlop on the rear, and Larry and CW had one Dunlop tire in the shop. We normally get about 8-10,000 miles on Dunlops. Before our trip, we were hoping to get a bit more from this other, more expensive brand. Unfortunately, we got about 4,600 miles – very disappointing.

We arrived at the Mayer dealership before they opened. We learned that Larry and my driver served in the 82d Airborne Division at Ft Bragg, North Carolina at the same time. They were in different units and didn't know each other. What a small world! Larry, CW and Jesus (that was the mechanic's real name!) had us on the road before noon. Those guys are totally pawesome!

With a new rear tire, we rode on a section of Highway 89A, which is, in my doggie opawnion, better than Tail of the Dragon in length, twisties, sweeps, and scenery, particularly on the section from Cottonwood through Jerome to Prescott Valley. We slowed down through the twisties because we frequently saw signs telling us to watch for someone named Falling Rock. He must have been climbing the sides of those mountains because he caused a lot of rocks to fall on the road.

We arrived in Irvine, California at night. Thomas had problems with the GPS taking us to the wrong place, so we stopped in a parking lot. He figured out how to get us to the hotel, and off we went. At the hotel, we talked about going to San Francisco before starting the eastward trek. We had not planned our return route, so we were flexible. Neither my driver nor Thomas looked at a map because they were comfortable with Thomas' GPS. They thought San Francisco was a few hours away from Los Angeles. Otherwise, if they looked at a map, they might have noticed that San Francisco and Los Angeles are a looooong day's ride from each other. My driver searched for a pet friendly hotel near San Francisco. He found one in Davis, which is beyond San Francisco. So, Davis became our destination for the next day.

We left the hotel early. We visited the Iraq/Afghanistan Memorial in Irvine. This is the memorial that Ol' Bill told us about. The real name of the memorial is the Northwood Gratitude and Honor Memorial. It had five pillars with the names of those killed in the Iraq and Afghanistan wars. Following each name is a number, which is their age. The names are in order of death.

Our original plan was to leave one of the Fallen Heroes rosters at The Wall in Washington, DC. After the Navy Seals facilitated the meeting between God and the leader of a terrorist organization in another country, we changed the route to take the Fallen Heroes roster to Ground Zero in New York City since our Fallen Heroes Roster begins after 9-11. However, after visiting the Memorial in Irvine, our perspective changed. My driver prayed for guidance. He felt Ground Zero is a memorial for those lost on 9-11, mostly innocent first responders and civilians. The Wall is for our Vietnam heroes. It now seemed inappropriate to leave an Iraq/Afghanistan Fallen Heroes Roster at either location, so we decided to bring the Rosters home and work with the Gold Star Mothers, Blue Star Mothers, and Operation Helping Hands for Heroes to determine a more appropriate presentation.

Northwood Gratitude and Honor Memorial, Irvine, California

After leaving Irvine, I sniffed the Pacific Ocean at Manhattan Beach State Park. My driver's dad and aunts grew up near that park. We rode up a portion of the Pacific Coast Highway and rode north to San Francisco. That's when my driver realized that San Francisco was a long day's ride, and Davis would make it be a bit longer.

We arrived near San Jose for fuel when the sun was starting to drop below the horizon. We had to roll through part of San Francisco to cross the Golden Gate Bridge. At traffic lights, hoomans in cars beside us would look at me and smile. There were lots of flashes from cameras. It was dark and drizzling when we rode across the Golden Gate Bridge.

We had a late night dinner at a hamburger place somewhere north of San Francisco. We arrived at the hotel in Davis around midnight. Thomas, my driver and I were tired. We didn't turn on the TV. In hindsight, they should have watched the weather forecast. My driver made reservations at a hotel in Ely, Nevada, and we went to sleep.

Manhattan Beach State Park, California

We woke up early, loaded up the bikes, mounted up and started our eastward trek. East of Sacramento, the road was a gradual uphill climb. We were headed towards Donnor Pass. We saw occasional signs that said something about "chains enforced". Chains? Soon afterwards, we ran into sleet, then a snow shower. We didn't know there was a forecast for snow. As we continued to roll, the snow was higher on the sides of the roads. My driver was talking with God and trying to figure out if we needed to turn around. We approached an exit, but the snow looked as if it was a few inches high on the road. My driver didn't think we could make it up the slope, so we continued rolling. At this point, we were rolling about 15 mph on the interstate. We pulled into a rest area, but didn't dismount. We noticed truck drivers putting chains on their truck tires. We tuned into an AM frequency on the radio that was broadcasting road conditions and weather information. The radio said that snow chains were required, but we noticed only a few cars seemed to be using chains.

My driver said he heard a voice say "I'll clear a path for you." I didn't hear anything. Maybe it came through the CB radio headset. Regardless, we were getting nervous, but we decided to push forward, pray for God's protection, and trust Him. As we rolled out of the rest area, our lower fairing was plowing about four inches of snow from the top of the snow on the road. That means we were rolling through about a foot of snow!

As we slowly rode out of the rest area at about 15-20 mph and in the merge lane, a truck passed us doing about 20-25 mph. We tucked in behind the 18-wheeler, which had chains. His tires cleared the snow and some of the slush. That section of road had a very rough groove, maybe from thousands of vehicles with chains. The road was rough, but it probably helped us with traction. We stayed in the rough groove mostly cleared by the truck ahead of us.

At one point, Thomas radioed us that he noticed we had a rooster tail as we rolled through the slush and packed snow. With the temperature dropping as we rolled uphill, he said he would tell us if he no longer saw the rooster tail. My driver thought if Thomas no longer saw the rooster tail, we would probably be on ice and sliding on the pavement before he could radio us.

We prayed for God to watch over us. We had a new rear tire that was mounted in Arizona. Isn't it cool how that worked out? Newer rubber in sloppy conditions. Coincidence? Maybe that was part of God's plan.

It took us over two hours to ride to the crest of Donnor Pass. On the other side of the pass, the roads were clear! We went from white being everywhere one minute, to earth tone colors the next.

In Nevada, we heard truckers on the CB radio talking about the two crazy idiots on the bikes riding through the snow. One of the truckers talked with us on the CB. He told us that he was impressed that we got our big bikes over the summit.

At the first exit in Nevada, we stopped at a gas station. We were there for about 30 minutes. Then, the snow flurries started falling. It was good to be on dry road again, so we decided to mount up to stay ahead of the snow.

We rolled through Fallon, Nevada, where my hooman uncle was born. The Loneliest Highway in the US (Route 50 through Arizona and Utah) is lonely, but scenic in a different kind of way.

While in the middle of nowhere, we stopped at the first gas station we saw. It looked like an old house with one gas pump in front of the house. We saw an old, above ground fuel tank. We weren't sure about the quality of gas and how long the gas had been setting in the tank. We saw a car parked by the house, but there were no customers. Thomas had his small gas can filled in the trailer, so we decided to take a chance and try to find another gas station. We eventually rolled into Austin, Nevada, and we were happy because we were very low on fuel.

We ran into snow showers again about 30 minutes from Ely. Visibility was low, but the snow wasn't sticking to the pavement, yet. I was glad when we rolled into Ely and there was still daylight!

At the hotel, we ordered pizza and chicken wings to be delivered. I ate a can of my MRE before dinner arrived. My driver took about six of the chicken wings, rinsed the sauce off, and pulled the meat off for me to eat as dessert. It was sooooo good! Thomas and my driver take good care of me.

In the desert, refuel when you can!

In looking for the next day's destination in Colorado, my driver remained concerned about bad weather in the mid-west.

This time, they watched some weather segments on TV stations while in the hotel. Before we departed for this adventure, we had a general contingency plan for weather. During our westward trek, the original contingency plan was that if we ran into bad weather while westbound, we would keep riding through it since weather fronts tend to move in a general eastward direction. If we were eastbound, we would decide whether to stay ahead of the weather and let it pass over us at night, or to hunker down for a day or two, let it pass, then stay behind it.

We left Ely and headed to Colorado. While driving through Utah, we saw a rainbow. It was odd. The rainbow wasn't arched toward the ground. It looked like smiling lips, as if God was smiling at us! My driver took a picture. After seeing that rainbow, we had no heavy rains, rough storms, snow showers or sleet during the rest of our mission. Coincidence? Maybe it was a sign of a blessing from God!

We rode through the Colorado Rockies. There was snow all around us, but the roads were clear. When we rode through northeast Colorado and into Nebraska, we had 40-60 mph crosswinds. Our bike stayed at about a 30 degree angle leaning to the left.

Snow on the ground through the Colorado Rockies, but the roads were clear

If we only had to deal with the wind, that would've been OK. But, we had to deal with dive bombing birds. These birds would gain altitude over the interstate median, then swoop down in front of us about two to four feet above the pavement. A few times, it appeared we were going to collide, but the bird would suddenly change angles and buzz us. Not only did my driver have the wind to battle and the dive bombing birds to avoid, I kept shifting around in my seat because I wanted to get a closer look at these crazy birds! We never saw such a thing and I would have loved to have sniffed one!

We visited the 20th Century Veterans Memorial in North Platte, Nebraska. I was barkless at how this one memorial covered all wars in the 1900's. We took pictures. After about 45 minutes at the memoria, we continued rolling eastward.

20th Century Veterans Memorial, North Platte, Nebraska

In Iowa, my driver had a run-in with a big ol' bug. I'm sure my riding friends can relate to this…. My driver saw this black dot hanging in the air ahead of us. Time seemed to shift into slow motion. The black dot got closer. It was a big, slow flying bug. We thought it was going to hit the windshield. The bug slipped over the top of the windshield and smashed into my driver's forehead at about eyebrow level above his sunglasses and below his helmet visor. I saw my driver's head snap back, heard him yell, and watched him use his left hand to wipe the bug juice from his forehead and glasses. His helmet got spackled with a few of the bug's friends. Not that it mattered, but we didn't know if they were kamikaze bugs flying head-on into us, or if they were trying to fly away from us and we smashed into their rear ends. First, dive bombing birds, then kamikaze bugs. What's with these creatures in the mid-west?

In Carroll, Iowa, we linked up with Bill Brown and his family, and with Terry and Zoe Ruchti. Bill is the Executive Producer of a 13-part TV series about the USO of North Carolina, the oldest USO in the USA. Bill's team completed the editing of the first show, which featured me. Terry and Zoe own Carroll Cycle Center (Harley-Davidson of Carroll), which is where we chillaxed for a few hours before having dinner with the Ruchtis and Browns. Thomas, my driver and I appreciate their pawspitality!

The next day, we continued our eastward journey towards Chicago. When we arrived at the Harley-Davidson shop in downtown Chicago, the ABC affiliate was waiting for us. We're not sure if we were on the news in Chicago, but we know some of the footage made its way to the ABC affiliate in Raleigh (WTVD). It was used in the Armed Forces Salute on Memorial Day that featured Thomas, my driver, the Patriot Guard, and me.

After seeing Lake Michigan in Chicago and watching the fog roll in, we headed south. We were homeward bound! We had reservations in Lafayette, Indiana. We stopped at a fast food chicken place near Rennaissance, Indiana, and the restaurant crew gave me a whole order of chicken strips – and then some!

When it got dark, I noticed lots of blinking red lights as far as my eyes could see. It was odd because the lights were all blinking in unison. On …… Off …… On ……. Off. The lights near us would go on and off at the same time as the lights far, far away. I shifted around in my seat to get a better sniff as we passed by some of the lights near the road. They were humongous properllers! Wind generators! Lots and lots of wind generators! I bet if we stopped on the side of the road near one of these towers and shut off the bike, we could probably hear the blades go whooooosh …….. whoooooosh ……… whoooooosh!

Eating dinner on the "Chuck Wagon", the nickname given to the trailer that Thomas pulled

We spent the night in Lafayette. When we checked out the next morning, one of the guests paid for our room. We asked if it was a mistake. The manager confirmed that our room was covered by a guest who wanted to remain anonymous. Thomas, my driver, and I were barkless over the kindness of a stranger. Whoever you are, thank you very much!

We stopped again in Maggie Valley, stayed at the Smoky Mountain Lodge, and had dinner at Smackers. We were tired and ready for our final leg.

My mom and a few friends met us at the Harnett County Veterans Memorial in Lillington, which was our start and end point. Our trip odometer read 7,927 miles – all to honor and remember our Fallen Heroes. We carried their names across the country for which they gave their lives. I hope the families of our

Fallen Heroes know that there are hoomans like us who try to remember their loved ones.

Throughout this mission, my driver had spasms in his neck and upper back that progressively got worse. It stems from the injury when we were hit in September 2009. My driver kept going by remembering that Jesus endured much greater physical pain for us, and our men and women in uniform endure hardships to protect us and ensure our freedom.

God created beautiful lands for us to enjoy. We had time for this trip because my driver was among the millions of unemployed Americans who were looking for work and who want to work. My driver thought about selling my Harley, but my mom and my driver made financial sacrifices to keep me in the saddle. I'm glad they did.

Before our journey, my driver prayed to God for help. Soon after, a person wanted to donate a few dollars towards gas, then another towards hotels. Initially, my driver declined the offers. My mom talked with my driver and asked if these hoomans could be the answer to prayers? My driver felt uneasy, and my mom said that perhaps sponsors feel blessed that they are a blessing to us. My driver and I prayed. My driver felt uncomfortable about sponsorship, but he opened up to it. Guess what? We had sponsors who helped us cover the hotel expenses on this mission, and for that, we are truly grateful! We appreciate the many hoomans who prayed for us. And, we hope they feel good about how we honored our Fallen Heroes.

The following are the sponsors of this mission and organizations that helped us during our mission:

Aiko Ewing (my hooman grandma)
Alan "Hillbilly" & Dee "One More" James
Angel de la Cruz
Ben Currin
Blue Star Mothers, Piedmont Triad Chapter 3
Brian & Barbara Tucker
Brunswick Air, Oak Island, North Carolina
Carroll Cycle Center, Carroll, Iowa
Catherine Cooper

Chicago Harley-Davidson Downtown, Chicago, Illinois
Chris & Caleb Rhew
Christine Distelhorst
Chuck "Greywolf" Ballas
Clark & Linda Steen
Colleen M. Sullivan
Connie & Wendell Harden
Dashboard Productions, Carroll, Iowa
Don "Aristocrat" Hacker
Dutch & Amy Macomber
Floyd & Brenda Baker
Grand Canyon Harley-Davidson, Mayer, Arizona
Hannah Stallings
Joe, Ruth & Jennifer Donnelly
Johnnie & Angie Norris
Keith & Peggy Zionts
Kentucky Fried Chicken, Renssalaer, Indiana
La Quinta Inn, Lafayette, Indiana
Margie Chaney
Marshall Porter
MeanStreet Riders
Melanie Spangler
Michael Brown
Mike Rogers
Monica Cash
Ol' Bill "Jammer" Amerson
Pam Brooks
Patty Bach
Paul Kolpel
Paul Sandler
Rich Lester
Richard Chowning
Roger Oakley
Rolling Thunder North Carolina Chapter 4
Rolling Thunder North Carolina Chapter 7
Shelia & David Sammons
Sheryl Emory
Smackers, Maggie Valley, North Carolina

Smoky Mountain Lodge, Maggie Valley, North Carolina
Terry Alexander
The Brown Family
The Family of Thomas Sanders
The Ruchti Family
Thomas Sanders
Tim & Chris Isaacs
Wingate by Wyndham, Destin, Florida
Wynne Vaughan

As with any cross section of patriotic Americans, there are bikers who are Christians, veterans, or who have big, caring hearts. You don't need to be a member of an organization, ride a motorcycle, or be a veteran to honor and respect our Fallen Heroes, our military, and our veterans. God Bless our Fallen Heroes, those serving now, those who served, their families and our allies.

Tongue in the Wind

Chapter 16: Offended

On a trip to South Carolina, we had to take a quick stop at a rest area on an interstate. We were on our way to stand in honor of Gunnery Sergeant Ralph Pate, a Marine who gave the ultimate sacrifice for our country. Since I tinkled at a gas station about 15 minutes prior to arriving at the rest area, I stayed in the saddle while my driver went to the restroom. We were parked in shade and I didn't indicate to my driver that I wanted to dismount. A man came up to me and started taking pictures. My driver returned. While putting on his headset, helmet, gloves, etc., this is how the conversation went (not verbatim, but accurate):

Man: I love your dog.

My Driver: Thanks.

Man: Can you remove that flag?

My Driver: What flag? (We were flying the US Flag, Christian Flag, and Honor & Remember Flag. The US funeral flag that was with us across the USA for our Fallen Heroes was on the luggage rack.)

Man: The flag with the cross.

My Driver: Noooooo. Those flags are staying on my Harley.

Man: That flag is offensive to me.

My Driver: (pause) (probably confused) So?

Man: This is a public area and I have the right to demand that you remove it or I'll report you to the authorities.

My Driver: My Harley is a private vehicle and I have the right to put anything on her just as you have the right to put bumper stickers and flags on your car to express your views, faith, or lack of faith. (pause) Can I pray for you?

Man: I really want a picture of your dog from this angle, but that flag is in the way.

My Driver: Crop it out because the flags stay, just like I'm not removing my T-Shirt or his helmet. (My driver was wearing a T-Shirt with a Red-White-Blue Cross and "In God We Trust" over the heart and pointed it out to the man. My driver also pointed out the Christian Flag sticker on my helmet before putting on my goggles and helmet.)

Man: (He said something, but my driver wasn't paying attention because he was putting on my goggles and helmet.)

My Driver: Did you serve?

Man: What do you mean?

My Driver: Did you serve our country in the armed forces of the United States?

Man: I don't believe in what we're doing over there. What does that have to do with this?

My Driver: I'm on my way to a funeral to honor a Marine who gave his life for our country in Afghanistan. What do you want me to do next, remove the decal on my fairing because it says "God Bless" the Marine?

Man: I hadn't noticed that, but yeah, can you? (After a few seconds) So are you gonna remove them so I can get my pictures?

My driver mounted our H-D, looked at the man, said "Nuts", and fired up the motor.

Man: What did you call me?   (I think he felt my driver insulted him; he seemed a little angry.)

My driver (Loudly over the pipes while he was backing out of the parking space): General McAuliffe. 101st Airborne Division. Battle of the Bulge. Google it. You might learn something about perseverance and sacrifice.

We rode away. I think that man wrote down our license plate number. Our license plate should be easy to remember.

My driver was not a happy camper. His neck and upper back was hurting, and this was the last thing he needed that day. He recently had a spinal injection and probably shouldn't have been riding because he had a spinal headache. I could tell he was mad because he was yelling profanity on the interstate. I never heard him do that. We took an exit to ride a back road to the staging area. There was no one behind us at the stop sign at the top of the exit. My driver bowed his head and asked God to forgive him. I think he prayed for that man in the rest area, too.

Fortunately, when we arrived at the staging area, we were among those who honor and respect our Fallen Heroes, those serving now, those who served, and their families – and we were among brothers and sisters in Christ. We bit our tongues on the topic and decided to cool down before barking about this so that we could try to stay objective and convey the conversation as accurately as possible.

After the mission, we rolled with Thomas Sanders and OB Jammer. On I-95 in South Carolina, OB's bike had a problem. Thomas, my driver, and I pulled over to stay with him. OB arranged for a truck with a rollback bed. He encouraged us to return home. We refused. You just don't leave a friend, biker brother, veteran brother, and brother-in-Christ behind.

The truck arrived. Thomas and I followed the truck to the Harley Davidson dealership north of Florence, South Carolina. We rolled through rain to reach the dealership. After OB was comfortable that his Harley-Davidson was in good hands for repairs, OB rode with Thomas. Thomas took OB to his house in "sunny Durham". We exited near Fayetteville to head home. What started as a frustrating ride to South Carolina ended with everyone arriving home safely.

After we returned home, my driver talked to my mom to vent a little. It was good that he took the Christian approach, even though he lost it for a few minutes on the road. Wow! I never heard of so many variations of that word that starts with the letter F.

Tongue in the Wind

Chapter 17: Charlie Mike II

Charlie Mike II occurred in mid-summer one year after the original Charlie Mike. The mission of Charlie Mike II was to honor our Fallen Heroes and veterans of the Korean War, sometimes referred to as "The Forgotten War". Like the original Charlie Mike, it was held by the Combat Veterans Motorcycle Association North Carolina Chapter 15-1.

The Korean War started a long time ago in doggie years. I got a short history lesson from driver. On a hooman calendar, it started June 25, 1950 when north Korea invaded South Korea. A cease fire went into effect on July 27, 1953. Technically, South Korea and north Korea are still at war because no peace treaty was signed.

This Charlie Mike had a special meaning to my driver. He served three years in Korea during the cease fire. It was supposed to be a one year assignment, but he kept getting involuntarily extended. He was assigned to a place called the "Western Corridor" for fifteen months. He returned to the US for a few months, and was sent back to Korea. He uses the small "n" when writing "north Korea" as a result of his experience.

Like the original Charlie Mike, this ride was certified for the IronButt Association's SaddleSore 1000. Most of the bikers rode for the mission. Those bikers viewed the IronButt recognition as an added bonus, rather than their purpose.

Chris "Gundy" Gunderson (rest in peace) was the Commander (Leader) of CVMA NC 15-1 and had overall responsibility for Charlie Mike II. "QuietMan" conducted the pre-ride safety briefing. "Cowboy" led the riders, families, and friends in prayer. God blessed us when he gave us Cowboy. Cowboy is a member of the Christian Motorcyclists Association and has a full-service motorcycle repair shop in his trailer: "Covered Wagon Services."

Jim Kazakavage flew a Gold Star flag on his yellow GoldWing, while his wife, Christi, was chauffeured by Ol' Bill "Jammer" from sunny Durham on his Harley-Davidson. I like to think that Jim's GoldWing is Gold, not yellow, because it is symbolic of the Gold Star. Christi is the Gold Star Mother of

Technical Sergeant Adam K. Ginett, US Air Force, killed in action on 19 January 2010 in Afghanistan.

On this mission, I brought the US flag that we carried across the USA a couple of months prior in honor of our Fallen Heroes. Thomas Sanders carried the Fallen Heroes roster from the Iraq and Afghanistan wars, a Christian Flag, an Honor and Remember Flag, and a Patriot Guard Riders flag. I wore the Gold Star bandana that I carried across the USA in memory of our Fallen Heroes and in honor of our Gold Star Mothers and families.

The original Charlie Mike had 14 bikes. Charlie Mike II had over 32 bikes. Fuz and Gail Melton rode from Martinsville, Virginia to be part of this mission. The Charlie Mike II route took us near their home!

Charlie Mike II Pre-Ride Group Photo

Because of the number of bikes, we were divided into two packs for safety. The first pack left late morning from the Harnett County Veterans Memorial in Lillington. They were led by "QuietMan". The second pack, led by "Schmuck", left about 20 minutes later. Gundy was the navigator in the first pack to guide them to a cemetery, which was our first destination. My driver and I were assigned to Schmuck's pack. My driver told me many times before we rolled: "Hey! We're Schmuckers! If we're with Schmuck, we've got to be good!" I gave him a curious look, perked my ears, and tilted my head. I think I heard that on television for a jelly commercial.

We arrived at the cemetery next to Lebanon Methodist Church in Mill Spring, North Carolina. We arrived at the cemetery shortly after the first pack departed. Gundy was there to meet us, read a citation, and then he returned to Lillington to prepare for the closing ceremony.

At the church cemetery lies Private First Class Bryant Homer Womack. One night during the Korean War, PFC Womack was the medic on a combat patrol. The patrol encountered a larger north Korean force. PFC Womack was wounded, but he tended to the other wounded soldiers. He was the last soldier to withdraw. He lost a lot of blood and collapsed. Soldiers came to carry him, and he died. PFC Womack was posthumously awarded the Congressional Medal of Honor. Womack Army Hospital on Ft Bragg is named after PFC Bryant H. Womack.

We departed Mill Spring and ran into rain in Charlotte. It rained so hard that there was standing water on the interstate. At about that time Ed "TailGunner" Williams' cruise control went out, so he had to hold the throttle with his hand.

We had problems with our engine shutting off when we were caught in Friday afternoon traffic near Shelby. At one point, our Harley-Davidson died while we slowed to a stop light. We were still coasting and my driver was trying to fire it up. We coasted off the road and the "Covered Wagon" pulled in behind us, along with Cowboy, Thomas Sanders, and our pack's tailgunner. My driver didn't want to give up and was able to fire her up. She would run OK at highway speeds, but would die in stop-and-go traffic. Cowboy and my driver talked over the CB and they thought we got a load of bad gas (gasoline, that is, not digestive). After two more refuels, my Harley was running fine and we were OK, except for my occasional personal gas blasts that my driver could smell. It probably came from eating too much of my duck and chicken jerky along with snacks shared by my biker friends at fuel stops. But, that's OK – it's all part of the expawrience!

We stopped for dinner on I-26 somewhere between Asheville, North Carolina and Johnson City, Tennessee. My driver prepared one of my cans of MRE. It was goooood! Since my driver was unemployed for over a year, he made sandwiches for him before we left and we carried them in a small cooler in the tour pack (trunk). He shared part of his sammich with me. We had bottles of water that my driver would refill at stops.

South of Johnson City, we ran into more rain. My driver didn't put on a rain suit. He got wet, but about 15 minutes after rolling out of the rain, he was dry again. Me? I just tucked in behind my driver, snuggled against his back, and I stayed dry.

We stopped for fuel on I-81 west of Natural Bridge, Virginia and had some overlap time with the first pack. We caught up with them, but we don't know if that was the plan. The first pack rolled out, and we stayed at the gas station for a bit longer. While at the gas station, Ed called Cowboy to load his bike into the trailer. Ed's cruise control was out, and all of the running lights on the backside of his Harley-Davidson Ultra were not working. He was having electrical problems and he felt that running dark was a danger. We rolled out of the gas station leaving Ed. That felt weird leaving one of our pack members behind. After the mission, Ed told us he grabbed a couple hours of sleep while waiting for Cowboy to arrive.

Before we left our house for this event, my driver did some research and figured out where we would cross the 38th parallel on I-81. When my driver saw the mile marker, he transmitted a very short message on the CB radio: "We just crossed the 38th parallel." There was silence, and we didn't know if anyone heard. Later, we learned that those with CBs heard. It was an unexpected transmission. It was sobering to them knowing that were riding for the Korean War Fallen Heroes and veterans and, geographically, we were parallel to north Korea.

We caught up with the first pack after midnight at around the junction of I-81 and I-66. At that point, we were a single, large pack.

We rolled into Washington, DC well after midnight. My driver took a pawesome photo of bike tail lights with the Washington Monument in the background. It was a bit shaky, but it was a pawesome photo. We arrived at the Korean War Memorial a couple hours before sunrise. We spent about 20 to 30 minutes at the Memorial, took some photos, then mounted up to ride south on I-95.

We ran into rain again south of Richmond and into North Carolina. We rode out of the rain by the time we arrived in Benson. We had humidity and partly sunny skies on the final leg from Dunn to Lillington. My driver and I had rain gear with us, which he calls sauna suits during the summer. With scattered thunderstorms during the summer, we carry our rain gear with us, but we usually prefer to get wet and cool off rather than put on our sauna suits. Me? I typically stay dry behind my driver.

Visiting the Korea War Memorial

In Benson, Wizard mounted flags on his bike. We rode to Dunn to link up with waiting friends and family. My mom and my driver's grandson, Chase, were also in Dunn to greet us. In Dunn, Harnett County Sheriff Deputies escorted the bikers, families and friends to Lillington.

After arriving in Lillington, Gundy led the closing ceremony and introduced us to Paul Hinkle, a Korean War veteran. CVMA NC 15-1 Auxiliary presented me with a custom bandana and made me an Honorary Mascot of the Auxiliary. After the closing ceremony and group photos, there were paw shakes, hugs, and ear scratches. Many went to the VFW post in Lillington, which had lunch waiting for us. It was hot and humid. I know I would not be allowed in the VFW post, so I took my driver home so he could give me a nice cool bath. I snoozed the rest of the day.

This was my second Charlie Mike, so my Iron Butt Association Membership (#35700) got another notch. My driver took about 800 photos, and we posted them on social media. In addition to me, there were other two-time Charlie Mikers: QuietMan, Glock, Wizard, Brian Volk, John and Paula Edwards, and my driver.

Posing with my CVMA NC 15-1 bandana

Chapter 18: Animal Protection

I took my driver to a lot of events. Most of the hoomans I meet are curious about me. We occasionally meet hoomans who do not like that I'm riding a motorcycle.

We attended a charity event in Raleigh one Saturday. There were lots of bikes there. There were also mounted law enforcement officers from Wake County, Cary, and Durham. They provided an escort to ensure the safety of everyone on the road who might come in contact with us. It's pawesome that I attended so many events that law enforcement officers in the area either met me or knew about me.

A lady walked up to my driver and politely asked if I am the dog riding on the motorcycle. My driver affirmed. She started yelling at my driver! She accused my driver of forcing me to ride against my will and exposing me to dangers. What the bark?? My driver replied that I enjoyed riding and that the dangers to me were no different than the dangers to him. She kept on talking through my driver's explanation, so I don't think she was listening.

When she told my driver that she is going to report him to the police, my driver calmly asked her to follow him. She asked "to where?" My driver replied that there were about a dozen police officers at the event, and that he was going to introduce her to them. She could choose the officer to file the complaint. Something happened to her face because she got red. I sensed she was angry. She yelled some bad words at my driver, then walked away on the sidewalk between the dealership and the street. She took a few steps, turned around and yelled more words that didn't sound nice. She took a few more steps, turned around, and yelled some more.

Sheeeesh!

Tongue in the Wind

Chapter 19: Gold Star Mothers

I feel honored to know many Gold Star Mothers, Fathers, Spouses, Children, and Siblings.

If you're unfamiliar with Gold Star Mothers, I'll take a moment to explain. I know I already barktated it, but I'll barktate it again. All Gold Star Mothers start as Blue Star Mothers. A Blue Star Mother is a mother who has a son or daughter who served or is serving in the armed forces. A Gold Star Mother is a mother who lost a child while in service to our country. The cause of death could be killed in action, but it can also be during training exercises, a traffic accident, or health-related condition. If the son or daughter was serving in the armed forces at the time of death, then the mother becomes a Gold Star Mother.

This may sound odd, but my driver and I actually met a couple of mothers who wished they were Gold Star Mothers. Some didn't have a child who served. I think maybe they don't understand what it means to be a Gold Star Mother. We asked one mother (who wasn't even a Blue Star Mother), and she told us that Gold Star Mothers get a lot of attention. My driver didn't know how to reply. If you ask any Gold Star Mother, they will probably tell you that they would not wish that designation on anyone.

My driver comes from a line of men who served. My driver served in the Army. My driver's brother and my driver's nephew served in the Army, too. My driver's dad served for 20 years in the Navy Seabees and served multiple tours in Vietnam. My driver's uncle served in the Navy Seabees. My driver's grandfather and great grandfather served in the Navy. That's about as far back as we can sniff my driver's family military service history.

My mom's father and her father's brothers served in the military. My mom's grandmother ("Big Momma") was a Gold Star Mother. Big Momma's son, Alvah Denton, was a staff sergeant in the Army Air Corps during World War II. His aircraft went down over water and the aircraft and the crew's remains were never found. One of the many reasons my driver honors Fallen Heroes is because of Alvah. Sadly, it seems that many in the current generations of my mom's family don't know about Alvah. A few said they "heard" something about a family member being shot down in WWII. A stone was placed at a church cemetery in memory of Alvah, and Alvah's name is on a memorial in the Harnett County Veterans Memorial in Lillington. What saddens us is the possibility of Alvah, and many men and women like him, being forgotten. That is one of the reasons my driver and I made tribute videos to honor Fallen Heroes. It's our way of helping hoomans remember so that our Fallen will not be forgotten.

Sniffing Alvah's name at the Harnett County Veterans Memorial, Lillington, North Carolina

I had been with my pawrents for about six and a half years. After the New Year, my driver and I helped the Gold Star Mothers, Blue Star Mothers, Rolling Thunder, Combat Veterans Motorcycle Association, Operation Helping Hands for Heroes, and other organizations to recover and honorably dispose of the wreaths from Wreaths Across America. During the wreath recovery, Julie Webb and Lori Southerland asked my driver if I could attend a Gold Star Mother meeting.

On the morning of the meeting, it was cold, but we rode the bike because that's what we do. My mom followed in the cage. We arrived at Julie's house for the meeting of the American Gold

Star Mothers – Dogwood Chapter. Julie has a dog and two cats, so I enjoyed sniff-learning about her furkids for a few minutes.

Before the meeting, my mom and my driver talked with Susan McClamrock and Christi Kazakavage, who talked about their sons. My driver was sitting on the floor, so I sat next to my driver so he could pet me and be comforted. I knew the conversation was bothering him.

My driver, my mom, and I were surprised when Paula Spivey presented me with a certificate making me an Associate Chapter Member in recognition of my service to our veterans and their families. At first, I was surprised because I'm a male and I don't have any puppies that I know of. I sniffed the certificate, which smelled honorable. They also gave me a Gold Star Mother coin and a white bandana with a gold star. Now, if anyone does a coin challenge with me, the GSM coin trumps any military coin out there! My driver and I were humbled by this honor.

It is an honor to provide comfort to Gold Star families. I just wish I could do more across the USA. My driver and I stood in honor of and escorted a number of Fallen Heroes. We met many Gold Star Families. I know there are moms around the world who lose a child, but, in my opawnion, only a Gold Star Mom knows how it feels to lose a child in the service of the country their child defended.

Our Fallen Heroes, which, in my doggie opawnion includes law enforcement officers and firefighters, and their families should be shown the utmost honor and respect for their sacrifices. The Patriot Guard Riders is oftentimes invited by families of the Fallen Heroes. You do not need to be a PGR member to honor and show your respect. It doesn't matter if you ride a motorcycle or drive a cage. The only requirement is the sincere desire to honor someone who gave the ultimate sacrifice.

What do we do during the funeral? To keep the explanation simple, we stand quietly in a flagline – each of us holds a US flag at the funeral home, church, or cemetery. Once the memorial service or celebration of life begins, we normally prepare to escort the hearse and family if there will be a procession to the place of interment.

At a military funeral, you will normally see me with my driver (or with one of my "road moms" if my mom is unable to attend) or mounted on my Harley-Davidson. If the passing results in a mother transitioning from Blue Star Mom to Gold Star Mom, I wear my Gold Star bandana. My driver and I eventually started making a custom bandana for each funeral I attended for a warrior who gave the ultimate sacrifice while in service to our country. Usually, a Gold Star Mom would remove the bandana from around my neck and present it to the new Gold Star Mom. It was an honor to be recognized by Gold Star families.

Some of the members of the American Gold Star Mothers Dogwood Chapter
Standing, l to r: Tammy Eakes, Susan McClamrock, Lorie Sutherland, Julie Webb
Sitting, l to r: Susan Badgley, Christina Kazakavage, Paula Spivey

I rode with the Patriot Guard a lot. But, several months after becoming affiliated with the Gold Star Mothers Dogwood Chapter, my driver and I withdrew from the PGR. However, our withdrawing was silent because we continued attending funerals, but as a repawsentative of the Gold Star Mothers Dogwood Chapter. Like most PGR members, we were there for one purpose: honor and respect.

There were incidences in which members (including at least one Ride Captain) publicly conveyed their dislike and disapproval of my presence at a funeral. They didn't seem to like a dog attending a military funeral or us taking pictures and videos to create tribute videos. Those few hoomans did not consider that Gold Star families appreciated my presence and the tribute videos we created in honor and remembrance of their sons and daughters, husbands and wives, fathers and mothers, brothers and sisters. On some missions, my driver and I were told that families specifically asked if I had arrived because they wanted to meet me. We did our best to stay low key because the focus should be on the Fallen Hero.

Keith Arbuckle and Bill Cook were the North Carolina leaders at the time. Keith, Bill and nearly every PGR member greeted me and checked on me during missions. They and several Ride Captains and Gold Star families came to our defense on social media and at missions, which, I believe, is one reason the Ride Captains at some missions would announce that my driver and I would be taking pictures with the family's consent. By then, most of the Ride Captains realized that what we were doing was respectful and appreciated by the families and friends.

Respect. It can be displayed in many ways. My driver noticed that at cemeteries, I refused to walk on the grass covering the vaults and caskets. I would walk between the foot of the grave and the head stones. Some PGR members noticed me doing that, too. Dee "One More" James was first to notice that I would drink water on the flag line, but I refused treats. My driver didn't train me to do that. I learned it by sensing my driver and becoming in tune with him.

My presence at PGR missions seemed to calm down around the time the Gold Star Mothers Dogwood Chapter named me an Associate Member. Several months later during the summer, I took my driver to a mission in Youngsville, North Carolina. My driver and I were in the shade on the other side of a truck with another PGR member. We listened to a group talk about how much money my driver and I were making on our videos, how one member went up the chain to put a stop to my activities with the PGR, and how another member was going to ban us from his missions when he becomes a Ride Captain. First, we made no money from our videos. Our videos were a reflection of our love, honor and respect.

After they ranted for several minutes, my driver and I walked to the other side of the truck, stopped and looked at them. They dispersed. I didn't recognize any of their scents, so they probably weren't familiar with the impact we have in trying to comfort grieving families and friends.

After this mission, my driver and barked it over with each other, and we silently withdrew from the PGR. We support their mission, but from that day forward, we attended missions with me representing the GSM chapter. We continued making custom bandanas for missions for Fallen Heroes and, in private after the funeral, a Gold Star Mother would remove the bandana from my neck and present it to the new Gold Star Mother. These are actions that Ride Captains witnessed and they saw firsthand the impact I have with hoomans. My driver and I didn't need to represent an organization – I was serving as an example of the unconditional love that comes from God.

The majority of the PGR members display honor and respect to the families and to each other. It only takes one bad peanut to destroy a batch of peanut butter. God was with us the whole time. He gave us the path to become lone wolves accepted by many organizations, rather than holding memberships. We don't need to be members of an organization to show honor and respect.

Chapter 20: USO Ambassadog

I was named one of the Ambassadogs for the USO of North Carolina. The USO was founded in North Carolina. USO-NC is the oldest, continuously operating USO in the USA. They do a lot to support our active military and their families. Some of you may know about them at airports, or free shows overseas for our military, sometimes in war zones.

My first event with USO-NC was a fund raiser that started and ended at Mudcat Stadium about 30 minutes east of Raleigh. There were several members of Rolling Thunder Chapter NC4 in attendance. That was a cool event and the Rolling Thunder Chapter President, Art Welch, suggested that his chapter lead the event in future years on behalf of USO-NC. Rolling Thunder made it happen. The annual event was moved to Ray Price Harley-Davidson in Raleigh, with Keith Parker planning the route and leading the bikes. Ray Price Harley-Davidson became the primary sponsor. The ride became known as the Freedom Ride.

When my driver was serving in the Army, he chilled between flights at the USO centers in major airports. When he was overseas one year, his commander volunteered him to be the escort officer for Miss USA, who was visiting South Korea on a USO tour. While overseas, he also attended concerts and shows sponsored by the USO.

The first year that the Freedom Ride was at Ray Price H-D, I met the reigning Miss North Carolina. Over the years, I met the next three Miss North Carolinas through USO-NC events.

During the reign of Brittany York as Miss North Carolina, she helped out Chase, my driver's grandson. Chase had a school project called Flat Stanley. He needed pictures of Flat Stanley taken at various places and with hoomans. Brittany helped us out and allowed us to take a picture of Flat Stanley with her and me. Brittany is pawruffic.

A few months later, USO-NC invited me to be part of the opening ceremonies at the Winston Salem Tennis Open. I had the pleasure of meeting several members of the North Carolina National Guard, a wounded Marine and being with Brittany again.

That was my first time on a pawfessional tennis court and at an opening ceremony. Neither my driver nor I knew what to do, so we just followed the cool bagpiper. I was careful not to mark anything.

At a few of the Freedom Rides, Keith asked us to be safety guards to work with the law enforcement officers to stop traffic for safety purposes. Being a safety guard allowed us pawtastic photo and video opportunities. Usually, the law enforcement support came from multiple departments, such as Wake County Sheriffs Department, Harnett County Sheriffs Department, Cumberland County Sheriffs Department, Coats Police Department, Lillington Police Department, Fayetteville Police Department, Apex Police Department, Angier Police Department and Cary Police Department. (I apawlogize if I missed anyone.)

One year, my picture was on the front of the official USO Freedom Ride tee shirt! How pawesome was that?!

For a couple of years, the USO held an ice cream event in Cary, North Carolina called Scoops for Troops. Patricia DeZetter and the USO volunteers put a lot of planning and effort into these events to show appreciation to our military. It was in the middle of summer. It was hot and humid, but there was a great turnout each year! Lumpy's Ice Cream gave me a free cup of ice cream to cool my tongue; they knew how to get to my heart.

At the second Scoops for Troops, we met Saskia Leary. At the previous year's event, Saskia took a picture of me. She submitted the photo in a contest and received the Hooman's Choice Ribbon. She used the photo on a greeting card, but she did not know how to reach me to get permission to use the photo. At the Scoop for Troops, she saw us again. She explained to my driver and me that she could not find how to contact me. She was apawlogitic. When she told us that the proceeds from the sale of the cards with my picture are going to the USO, my driver and I looked at each other. My driver told her she had our blessing because her heart was in the right place! She had a check to present to the USO. Saskia and I posed with a few USO volunteers for the check presentation.

Saskia loves the US military. We learned of her story through Anna Martin of the USO. You see, Saskia was born in The

Netherlands, or some pawple call that country Holland. She lived there when Germany occupied her country. She remembers when the US military liberated her country. She continues to respect and love our men and women who are willing to give their lives for the freedom of citizens of other countries!

To Saskia and all the USO staff and volunteers: Thank you for supporting our military service members through your time and actions!

Saskia and her People's Choice winning photo

Tongue in the Wind

Chapter 21: Ride across the USA II

My second ride across the USA had several objectives. (1) Carry a Fallen Heroes Roster from the Kipling Cross in Kipling to the Iraq/Afghanistan War Memorial in Irvine, California. (2) Increase awareness of the American Gold Star Mothers organization. (3) Fly the POW/MIA flag across the USA and to Rolling Thunder in Washington, DC in support of releasing Sergeant Bowe Bergdahl.

SGT Bergdahl was captured by the Taliban and became listed as a Prisoner of War (POW) by the Department of Defense. Our mission regarding SGT Bergdahl was not a political statement. It was simply helping Americans to be aware that an American soldier was being held in captivity by the Taliban. I realize there was controversy about how he was captured and why. Since SGT Bergdahl was officially listed as a POW, we simply tried to help people become aware that the Taliban had a US soldier as a POW. Anything beyond that can be sorted out by the military.

On this adventure, we met hundreds of hoomans. Two hoomans knew about the Gold Star Mothers organization, but we met no one who knew about SGT Bergdahl's captivity.

Our previous trip had some publicity with coverage from newspapers, radio, and local television news. Thomas' bike wasn't running, so rather than delaying this trip, my driver and I barked it over and we decided to go solo with God watching over us. We decided to update my social media page, but we would not actively engage the press. If the press contacted us, we would be courteous. It was a good decision to go solo with God because we witnessed several blessings.

Our mission was affiliated with Operation Helping Hands for Heroes or "OHHH". I started my cross-country mission with OHHH's "Ride for the Warrior" that started and finished in Fayetteville. I didn't count the number of bikes on my paws, but there were lots of bikes! After the ride portion of the event, Donna Taylor gave my driver and me a bandana that was blessed in Israel. One side has Psalm 91 embroidered in Hebrew. The other side has Psalm 91 embroidered in English.

After the Ride for the Warriors, my driver went to his church to meet and listen to Peter Loth, one of the youngest survivors of the WWII Holocaust. My driver took the Psalm 91 bandanas with him to church. During the introduction of Mr. Loth, Barry Battelstein read Psalm 91. My driver told me that he was so shocked that his jaw dropped. After the service, Barry gave my driver a copy of a book about Psalm 91. His jaw dropped again! Was this a coincidence? Since we would be solo without Thomas Sanders as our wingman, was this God using other pawple to let us know loud and clear that He is with us?

On the first day of our westbound trek, we stopped at Morrow Mountain State Park near Albemarle. That was one of Lyle Davenport's favorite destinations. We stopped there in memory of Lyle. We intended to stay a few minutes, but hoomans saw me and started talking with us and asking questions. My driver gladly talked about our mission and how we believe that God was blessing us through the mission.

Visiting Morrow Mountain State Park, North Carolina

We stayed in rain from Charlotte to north of Columbus, Georgia. As long as we're rolling, I stay dry by tucking in behind my driver. East of Atlanta, the traffic came to a stop. The rain was coming down hard. Without us rolling, I was getting soaked. My driver wore his rain suit, but his clothes under the rain suit were already soaked. He didn't wear boot covers, so water came up the pant leg to soak his pants, and water came down through the opening around his neck to soak his shirt. When we were about 30 minutes from Columbus, the skies became blue. We found a place to park so my driver could take off the rain suit. By the time we arrived an hour later at my hooman grandma's and uncle's house in Columbus, we were dry!

Taking a snooze while refueling under an awning

We spent the next day in Columbus. There were two furkids in the house: Bella and Frisco. It was sunny, comfortable temperatures and low humidity. I took my driver for three walks that day! I also learned to use a doggy door; I'm a quick learner. Bella is a pug and Frisco is a miniature poodle. The doggy door was the right size for them. I had to squeeze and wiggle my way through, but once my tail went through, I looked at my driver with a "Taa-daa!" look. I had fun going through the door and my driver would watch my tail disappear through the door, then see my head coming through the door a few seconds later. To me, it was like a game.

The following day, we rolled into Alabama towards Montgomery. It was foggy so we rolled slower than usual. We arrived at the Tuskegee Airmen Museum before they opened. We forgot about the time zone change when we rolled into Alabama from Georgia. We arrived an hour ahead of plan from a clock pawspective.

The interior of one of the hangars was under construction to convert it to a museum. It had an original P-51 Mustang "Red Tail" suspended in the hangar and covered with plastic to protect it from the sheet rock dust. The P-51 was not yet available to the public. After spending time with the construction crew and explaining our mission, we were honored and humbled that the construction foreman allowed us to see the aircraft and take photos. The construction crew told us they had the honor of meeting the fighter pilot of that particular aircraft: Captain Les Williams.

Pawsonally checking out a P-51 in Tuskeegee

Between Montgomery and Mobile, we came upon a truck driver southbound towards Mobile. My driver and the truck driver talked on the CB. The truck driver was from Four Oaks, North Carolina. My driver told the trucker that he and I were in Four Oaks to honor a Fallen Hero named Jeff Sherer. The trucker asked if we heard of a dog named Chewy. My driver replied, "This is Chewy on the bike!" What a small country! The truck driver phoned a friend who attended Freedom Biker Church. He radioed us that his friend was excited that we crossed paths on the road. Coincidence? My driver and the trucker talked on the CB for several minutes. We were rolling faster than the trucker. With the rolling hills south of Birmingham, it didn't take long before we were out of CB radio range.

We rolled into Battleship Park in Mobile in the early afternoon. It was warm and humid, but it was refreshing to stretch our legs, drink some water and sniff around the various memorials. The Working Dog Memorial is pawesome! There are a set of paw prints next to a set of hooman jungle boot prints. Those paw prints are life-sized, but they look huge! I have huge paws to fill, and I hope I was doing an OK job.

Military Working Dog Memorial, Mobile, Alabama

At Battleship Park, we met a family visiting the USS Alabama as an educational trip. We spent about 30 minutes with the family and several more visitors. We eventually mounted up and rolled west.

POW/MIA Memorial, Mobile, Alabama

Our journey across Mississippi and Louisiana was uneventful. In East Texas, we took a detour to visit the battleship USS Texas. It felt very humid. There were humongous mosquitoes everywhere! We didn't stay long. We posed for a photo in front of the battleship, used the restroom, and stopped at a distance to look at the San Jacinto monument. San Jacinto is where the Texas army under the command of Sam Houston defeated Santa Anna's army. After the short stop at the monument, we continued our westward trek.

At every stop during our journey, pawple came to us to meet me and talk with my driver about me. As a result, we could never plan on short refuel stops or stopping at a rest area just to empty our bladders and roll. We were on God's time! My driver didn't wear a watch on this trip. We used the sun to estimate the time of day.

USS Texas

When we stopped in Kerrville, Texas for the night, we heard an occasional noise. It is hard to describe, but it sounded like a chirp and clatter. We only heard it sometimes when we were stopped and idling. Since most of our time was rolling at highway or interstate speeds, the wind noise probably masked the chirping and clattering. In the hotel parking lot, my driver looked over the bike. I sniffed the bike in various areas to help him find the source of the noise. We didn't find anything odd.

San Jacinto Monument

My driver went to school in South Texas. He was somewhat familiar with Kerrville. Although he never lived in Kerrville, he told me several times that we are in Texas Hill Country and we need to watch for deer. My observation is that it seems like they roll up the sidewalks a few hours before sunset.

When we stopped in Kerrville, Texas for the night, we heard an occasional noise. It is hard to describe, but it sounded like a chirp and clatter. We only heard it sometimes when we were stopped and idling. Since most of our time was rolling at highway or interstate speeds, the wind noise probably masked the chirping and clattering. In the hotel parking lot, my driver looked over the bike. I sniffed the bike in various areas to help him find the source of the noise. We didn't find anything odd.

My driver went to school in South Texas. He was somewhat familiar with Kerrville. Although he never lived in Kerrville, he told me several times that we are in Texas Hill Country and we need to watch for deer. My observation is that it seems like they roll up the sidewalks a few hours before sunset.

The next morning felt cool and refreshing, as compared to the humidity in Alabama, Mississippi and Louisiana. West of

Kerrville, the speed limit became 80 mph. We were curious as to what my slobber would do at that constant speed. The scenery seemed like the same brush on both sides of the interstate, but we were in the Hill Country – and the roads on those hills have long upward and downward slopes.

Speed limit through West Texas

At a rest area near Sonora, Texas, we met two vans of geology students from Beloit College in Wisconsin. They were going to Big Bend to study rocks. I wasn't interested in their topic, so I grazed on grass. My driver was talking with the students, but he would frequently look back to me and tell me to stop eating the grass.

About 30 minutes after being back on the road, the grass in my stomach was starting to get to me. My driver noticed some thicker-than-normal slobber floating forward and sticking to the back of the windshield. There was an occasional piece of grass with the slobber.

The speed limit was 80 mph and we had a head wind. A few minutes after my driver noticed the grass sticking to the back of the windshield, I puked. I took a couple of heaves, with the first heave being smaller than the last. There was grass mixed in with the slime. The glob floated forward as a spread-out, floating stream of goo. Some of it dropped onto the tank and my driver's legs. Some of it landed on my driver's shoulder and neck. Some of it floated forward and stuck to the back of the windshield. A glob of it was pushed up by the air flow coming from under the fairing. That glob was pushed up to the air flow coming over the top of the windshield. My driver saw it and was trying to figure out what it was, while also trying to process that his shoulder, neck and parts of his pants were now wet. His mouth was open because he was trying to tell me something. That grassy glob of liquid landed on my driver's face and some of it went into his mouth. He started having heaves. We quickly stopped on the shoulder. We decelerated so quickly that I was scrunched up against my driver's back. My driver quickly dismounted and had several dry heaves. He walked around a little, wiped his face, had more dry heaves, and checked on me. I was feeling fine at that point! My driver had a lot of slobber coming out of his mouth. He was spitting, coughing, and gagging. Hey! He was acting like me!

About a mile east of Van Horn, Texas with the speed limit at 80 mph, we quickly developed a wicked vibration in the handlebars. It was scary! My driver slowed down and took the Van Horn exit. When we slowed, the vibration seemed to disappear. We rolled into a Love's truck stop.

My driver and I dismounted. He used his fingers to feel the top of the forks behind the fairing. He told me that he was looking for any sign of a leak from the forks. He helped me dismount, and I tried to help him. I sniffed the bottom right fork and looked at my driver. He knows that look on my face. He asked me what I sniffed. I sniffed the bottom of the fork again and looked at him. He came to check it out and found the forward nut on the right side axle clamp was about to drop from the bolt stem. The rear nut was finger tight. He checked the left fork, which has a two-part bushing and a bolt that goes into a hole in the bottom of the left fork to secure the rotor cover. The bolt and bottom half of the bushing was missing!

Prior to our mission, we took our bike to an independent shop in Fayetteville to replace both tires and for routine service. At the truck stop in Van Horn, my driver thought the person probably couldn't figure out how to reassemble the rotor covers. Even more dangerous, it appears he forgot to torque the nuts on the axle cap!

That could have cost us our lives if it all came apart on the interstate!

A truck driver let us borrow a torque wrench for the axle clamp nuts. We rolled to the NAPA auto parts store in Van Horn. We had a choice. Either my driver figure out how to put it back together, or find a rental truck and head home. Rather than giving up and loading the bike on a rental truck and taking her home, we spent a lot of time working on the left fork in the West Texas heat. The guys in the parts store were helpful when my driver needed different sized nuts and bolts to figure out how to improvise the hardware for the rotor cover. They also let us borrow a torque wrench and some tools that my driver didn't have in his tool bag. With my supawvision, my driver improvised a rotor cover mount. He rechecked the torque at a lot of places around both wheels. He found some that were tight, but less than what he estimated the torque to be. We were able to continue our mission. God's angels were watching over us as promised in Psalm 91!

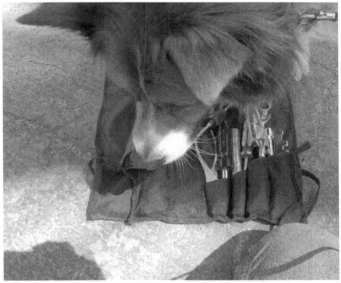

Helping my driver with roadside repairs in Van Horn, Texas

When we rolled into El Paso, we stopped at Barrett Harley-Davidson. Some of the staff saw me ride into the parking lot, and told my driver I could go inside with him to get out of the heat. We went to the parts counter. They were very helpful. In order to get the mounting hardware, we would have to buy the whole rotor cover kit. My driver was confident that his improvised repair would get us across the country and back.

We talked with a service technician, who looked up the torque specifications of various bolts around the front wheel and rear wheel. It turns out that my driver's guesses were close! We borrowed a torque wrench and rechecked the torques at multiple places. We both felt better.

We arrived at our hotel in Deming, New Mexico much later than expected. My driver told me that the next day was going to be long. He was looking forward to the next day because he would be in a familiar area in Arizona – Ft Huachuca, Sierra Vista, Tombstone and Bisbee. Ft Huachuca was my driver's regimental home. This was my first time visiting these places!

After entering Arizona, we stopped at a rest area that had lots of humongous boulders! I walked my way up some boulders while my driver stayed on the ground. When I got to the top, I did a Rin Tin Chewy pose for my driver to get a picture. There was no grass at this rest area, just lots of rocks and dirt. I went to the doggie area and sniffed peemail and left some replies to let others know that I was there.

Posing on a rock in Arizona

132

In Tombstone, we visited Boothill Cemetery. We rode slowly down Allan Street, and we saw the OK Corral from a distance. It was a dry heat, and my driver wanted to keep rolling so I would stay cool The short ride from Tombstone to Bisbee was interesting. As we rolled on the mountain road, the scenery changed from desert brush to trees. The temperature seemed much cooler. I was feeling comfortable. We rolled through a tunnel. My driver told me that we were rolling into Bisbee. We exited the highway, and rolled through a winding road with houses built along the mountain side. It was pawesome!

Entering Bisbee, Arizona

After visiting Bisbee for about an hour, we rolled to Sierra Vista. It got hot again. We stopped at a doggie grocery store so we could reload my supply of treats. My driver wanted to roll onto Ft Huachuca, but with the heat, he didn't want to spend time putting on riding gear that would be required on the Army post. So, we rolled by the main gate, my driver saluted, I sniffed the air, and we rolled to Huachuca City, Patagonia, and Tuscon. I sensed that my driver was very happy to be in his regimental home state and riding on roads very familiar to him.

On our way to Yuma, we stopped in Casa Grande for dinner. There were lots of flies! I mean, not just a lot, but a whole LOT! We tried to eat dinner in the parking lot, but there were just way too many flies. I was able to eat my dinner, but my driver gave up eating his. We mounted up and rode into the sunset towards Yuma. We arrived at our hotel late at night. My driver looked at the Harley-Davidson map to estimate when we would arrive at our destination on the next day. We both bathed that night. It felt good to be a clean doggie.

Rolling through southeast California was interesting. It looked like an endless hilly, sandy beach, but no water. When we rolled through a mountain range and stopped in Alpine for fuel, my driver had to put on his light Harley-Davidson jacket.. The cooler air and low humidity was refreshing. We stayed in Alpine for about an hour. We both took a short nap on a picnic table in the shade. My driver woke up because he was shivering. If he didn't get cold, we would have probably slept most of the day!

We arrived at the Northwood Gratitude and Honor Memorial in Irvine, which we refer to as the Iraq-Afghanistan War Memorial. This memorial has 20 panels. The panels have the engraved names of all those who gave their lives in the Iraq and Afghanistan Wars. We took several pictures. We took photos of the panels, and close up photos of many names. The names are in order of death. Our Fallen Heroes Roster had the dates of death of each Fallen Hero. We looked up the names of those we knew from attending their funerals, a Flags for Fallen Military ceremony in their honor, or an event in their honor. Finding each name on a panel took a lot of time because we had to find the panel's year, then scan across each row until we found the name.

Northwood Gratitude and Honor Memorial

I sniffed one name on a panel, sat, and looked at my driver. I sniffed it again and look at my driver again. My driver saw the name: Samuel Griffith. He asked me "Who's that?" I sniffed the name again. He told me "I never heard of Samuel Griffith." I sat and looked at him. He took a close-up picture of the name. He knew nothing about Samuel Griffith.

My driver continued looking up names. I was dragging my driver's leash around while I sniffed the pillars. I looked up at another panel and waited for my driver to notice. When my driver came into view, I sat and stared at an area of a panel, then looked at my driver, looked at the panel again, and looked at my driver again. My driver put a finger in the area and moved his finger to different names asking me "Here? Here? Here? Here?" I gave him a low "woof" and he stopped on a name. He took a close-up picture of that name: Christopher Adlesperger. Like Samuel Griffith, Christopher's name was completely unfamiliar to my driver.

After leaving the Memorial in Irvine, we rolled into a cemetery in Ingleside. Before our mission, my driver contacted the cemetery and received the location of his grandfather. We stopped at a section of the cemetery and we dismounted. My driver walked quickly and was scanning headstones. He found James Ewing, his grandfather. He sat on the grass in front of the headstone. He was quiet. I sensed something different about him. I leaned up against him. He started talking to someone, but it wasn't me. I think he was talking to his grandpa. My driver thanked his grandpa a lot. My driver told his grandpa that he was the first person who ever protected my driver from his dad. My driver's grandpa passed away from cancer when my driver was about 10 years old. The last time my driver was in this cemetery was during the funeral. Then, while talking, my driver started crying and saying "I love you, grandpa". He said it many, many times while kneeling on the ground. I leaned harder against my driver. He cried for a long time. Then, all of sudden, he stood at attention, saluted, and said "Thank you, grandpa!" He held the salute for a long time. I leaned against his leg so he could feel me. He then got on his knees, wrapped his arms around me, and thanked God and thanked me. I didn't know what he was thanking me for. We're best friends. He's my hooman dad. I'm his furchild. We're PTSD Battle Buddies for life.

Visiting my hooman great-grandpa

My driver and I went back to the bike to get a small urn that had part of his dad in it. We returned to his grandpa. My driver kneeled on the grass in front of the head stone and set the little urn on the headstone. He said "I forgive you, dad." Then he thanked his grandpa some more. I leaned against my driver and he put one arm around me while he cried. My driver stuck one of my mission dog tags into the ground next to the headstone. We took some pictures, then mounted up. I think we were with his grandpa for almost two hours.

We stayed with my Great-Aunt Connie and Great-Uncle Wendell in Camarillo. They took us to the Veterans Memorial in Camarillo, then to Santa Barbara where we chilled and had lunch overlooking the Pacific Ocean.

At the Santa Barbara Pier, I sniffed a lot of high-end dogs. I mean, some of their hiney ends were high in the air. They looked to have a good bloodline, compared to the mutts like my driver and me. I also put my paws on an area of the pier so I could get a better view of the ocean.

On the way back to my great-aunt's and great-uncle's house, we stopped at a roadside area for pictures. Wendell and Connie told us that they camped in that area, so they were familiar with that stretch of the beach.

Wendell, Connie, me and my driver

After we returned to the house, we spent time "watching" the solar eclipse, which was visible on the west coast. We spent two nights with my great-aunt and great-uncle, and they truly are great! It felt good to be with family. My driver told me he has another cool aunt and cool uncle in Oregon named Marcia and Marshall. The last time my driver saw his aunts was when my driver's grandmother went to Heaven when my driver was in college. That would be over 200 years in doggie years! Wow, my driver is ancient!

On the first leg of our eastward trek, we stopped at the President Ronald Reagan Library. The location seemed to be less than 30 minutes from my great-aunt and great-uncle's home. President Reagan was the President when my driver started his military service. On the street that enters into a loop in front of the entrance, my driver dismounted. He stood at attention, said "Thank you, Mister President", and saluted. I wanted to dismount, sniff around, and leave some peemail, but my driver said we are here to render our respect, not render our pee.

We rolled back to the interstate to continue our eastward trek. We were on a very rough portion of Route 66. The pavement was in good shape, but there are a lot of little dips and rises. At 55 mph, the bike's shocks were stretching and then being forced to compress hard. My driver slowed down a bit and put his feet on the highway pegs. He saw something shiny spinning in the rear view mirror. He put his feet on the floorboard and realized the right floorboard was missing. The floorboard pan was there, but the floorboard was missing.

We slowed down, turned around, and went to the approximate area where we thought he saw the flying, shiny object. Sure enough, the floorboard was in the dirt on the eastbound side of the highway. My driver squeezed the floorboard between his backrest and my saddle. I sniffed the floorboard to make sure it wasn't going anywhere.

Somewhere east of Borax, California (I think)

We rode several miles and came to an intersection. We could have continued straight, but we decided to park in the shade under the overpass to figure out how to do an expedient roadside repair. It was a hot, dry heat. After we drank water, I sniffed the floor pan while my driver held the floorboard and looked at the pan. He opened the tour pack. He found spare boot laces, but kept digging.

He found the 100 mph table (duct tape). He wrapped tape around the floorboard and pan. He used the boot laces to wrap around the floorboard and floorpan. That floorboard wasn't going anywhere!

My driver put things back into the tour pack while I left a short peemail. We fired up the motor and continued straight. About 20 minutes later, our low fuel light went on. My driver and I realized that we had not seen any Route 66 signs. Somehow, we rode into the Mojave Preserve and had not seen a car since leaving the overpass. My driver pulled off the road to get the map. He could see the Mojave Preserve on the map, but no roads were on the map. We barked it over. We had not seen a gas station since the last time we filled up, so going back was not a good idea. He mounted up, fired up the motor, and, this time, he kept the bike at about 50 mph to try to conserve fuel.

We saw a sign for Kelso Depot about 20 miles ahead, but there was no service – no gas station! It was 55 miles to Baker. We had lots of water with us, but we estimated we had fuel for about 30-40 miles. My driver started talking with God. On downhill slopes, he put the bike in 6th gear at 55 mph. On the uphill slopes, he put it in 5th gear at about 45-50 mph. We had a tail wind. We rolled into Kelso Depot. Sure enough, no gas station. We kept rolling.

I think we're lost!

Northeast of Kelso Depot, my driver turned the squelch low on the CB radio. We could hear some chattering on the CB radio. It sounded like several truck drivers having an important conversation. My driver didn't want to waste any fuel by stopping, so he was scanning the horizon looking for signs of roads or the sun reflection from windshields. We were thinking we were a few miles from an interstate. After a few minutes, there was nothing on the CB except static. We somehow missed the signs to Baker. We found ourselves rolling into Searchlight, Nevada. As the bike rolled onto the gas station pavement, the bike began sputtering and popping. We coasted to the gas pump.

We refueled, drank lots of water, and licked ice cream to cool off. There was a patch of cool, green grass at the back of the gas station, but there was a sign that read "Stay Off Grass", so we respected the hooman rule.

My driver and I thought about the past hour. We think he should have done a u-turn under the overpass where we secured the floorboard to the floorpan. That would have kept us on Route 66. We were supposed to be riding through Needles, California, but were 50 miles off-course to the north.

We rode south through Laughlin and Bullhead City, where the temps were near 115. It was hotter than I have ever been. In Bullhead City, we saw a sign for Route 66 and decided to follow it east. That was a slow, but pawruffic section of road! We rode through Oatman and saw loose donkeys. We rode twisties, some of which had no guard rails.

It was dark when we rolled into Ash Fork, Arizona. We were both hungry, but we didn't see any open convenience stores or fast food places. We rolled into a gas station to fill-up. The restaurant part of the gas station was closed. My driver opened a can of my MRE and put it in my travel dish. I was hungry, but I looked at my driver. He told me to go ahead and eat. I looked at my dinner and looked at him. I knew my driver was hungry, and drinking water wasn't going to be enough for him. He told me he had something to munch on. He opened the tour pack and took out a granola bar. He told me to eat, but I kept looking at him. He unwrapped the granola bar and took a bite. I was satisfied that he had something to eat, so I ate my dinner. While I was eating, he knelt next to me, patted my back, and said "Thank you, Chew-Chew."

We arrived in Flagstaff, Arizona about eight hours behind schedule. We had not uploaded any pictures from the camera to the laptop since Yuma, but we were tired. While my driver searched for a hotel and made online reservations for Tucumcari, New Mexico, I slept next to him.

In the morning, we woke up a little later than normal. Before checking out of the hotel, we huddled and my driver prayed. We prayed every evening to thank God for the safe adventure, and we prayed every morning asking for His guidance and for His hand of protection. After getting lost and nearly running out of fuel, my driver prayed for encouragement and a sign that we are doing what He wants us to do. He told God he trusts Him.

We checked out of the hotel and rode to a gas station near the hotel. After refueling, my driver exited the back of the gas station into a parking lot. On the right, we saw a huge trailer: "Positive. Encouraging. KLOVE". That was sooooo pawesome! We prayed for encouragement. God gave us a HUGE sign – with real words. KLOVE is one of the stations we search for frequently on the radio. My driver said he could sense God smiling at us. God has a pawruffic sense of humor!

We rolled up to the truck and there was no one there. My driver dismounted, and we took pictures and selfies with the KLOVE trailer in the background. We waited for a few minutes, but the crew was either in the hotel or in the restaurant. We decided to roll.

KLOVE trailer in Flagstaff, Arizona

We visited Meteor Crater. Dogs are strictly not allowed. The person at the ticket booth asked about me, so we explained our mission. She explained that Meteor Crater is privately owned. She talked with Lanah at Bar-T-Bar Ranch to explain our mission. When Lanah met us, she asked if were the ones with the list of Fallen Heroes. She led us on a short hike to the crater's rim. I had to keep my driver on his leash. If my driver visited without me, he would have seen the crater from a building. With me, he had the honor of standing on the rim with me. It was a great moment to share. We took photos of the Gold Star Rosters on the rim of Meteor Crater. Some hoomans may view this as a hole in the ground, but I highly recommend visiting. But, please remember, no pets are allowed.

Meteor Crater, Arizona

We visited the Petrified Forest National Park. When we arrived, our original plan was to take a few pictures and continue our eastward trek. We decided to ride the 20 mile road to the other end, then back to the park's main entrance. That was soooo pawsome looking at petrified wood older than my driver. My driver wouldn't let me dismount to sniff or pee on any of it until after we returned to the park's entrance and gift shop building.

Petrified Forest National Park, Arizona

Somewhere in eastern Arizona, our cruise control went out. We wanted to "stand on the corner in Winslow, Arizona", but I think we rolled past the exits when my driver was focused on the throttle. Rather than spending time in the heat to sniffestigate the problem, we decided to wait until we reached Tucumcari.

Before reaching Albuquerque, my driver's wrist was getting tired. Now, let's flash back for a moment. We have a friend, Ed "TailGunner" Williams, who passed away a couple of months before this adventure. Over a year ago, we rode with Ed and over 40 bikers in the Combat Veterans Motorcycle Association NC 15-1 Charlie Mike II. During that ride, Ed's cruise control went out. So, let's return to us in New Mexico.

While riding through Albuquerque, my driver remembered that when Ed's fuse burned out during Charlie Mike II, it took out his cruise control and his rear lights. We were about an hour or two from sunset. My driver was ciphering in his head to estimate the next fuel stop. We could check the fuse at the stop. He estimated about 45 minutes.

We came up on an exit and he heard Ed's voice through the headset say "Take the exit ... Now! Now! Now!" Was it Ed or was it someone on the CB? We're not sure. We braked hard into the exit, which dumps onto a service road. We stopped at the only place on the mountainside: Sedillo Hill Travel Center, which was closing in about 15 minutes. My driver fueled the bike and went into the store to use the restroom and buy some water before working on the bike.

James Baca and his father talked with my driver while he was in the store. It turns out that James was the wrestling coach for PFC Christopher Adlesperger, USMC, who was killed in Iraq. Mr. Baca knows Christopher's mother. He asked to look at the Fallen Heroes Roster. It was a pain to pull it out of the saddlebag and repack it, but it was worth it.

Mr. Baca and my driver had an emotional moment when they saw Christopher's name. He took my driver into the store to show him a picture of Christopher on the store's wall. James' parents own the store and I think he stops there after school to visit and help out. My driver and I gave Mr. Baca a mission dog tag to give to Christopher's mother. Mr. Baca's parents hugged my driver and told him that God sent him.

Mr. Baca and his father asked us if we knew what my name means in Spanish. Mr. Baca told my driver it means "Jesus". My driver lived in Texas as a teenager. He remembered. My driver told James that my name is spelled c-h-e-w-y, not c-h-u-y.

After they closed the store, my driver and I removed the side panel to access the fuses. My driver pulled the fuse to the cruise control. I sniffed the fuse to check it. It was blown. We carried spare fuses and bulbs. My driver replaced the fuse. He fired up the bike and the lights on our rear end lit up.

With no one around, my driver was very emotional. He cuddled with me in that empty parking lot for about 15 minutes.

We continued our eastward trek. Our cruise control worked again.

In Tucumcari, my driver uploaded the pictures from the camera's memory card. He began clicking through the pictures from Irvine. Then he saw the close-up photo of the name I looked at on the panel: Christopher Adlesperger. My driver's jaw dropped. He looked at the laptop screen, then he looked at me. He asked me "Chewy, how did you do this." I calmly looked at him and casually panted. He then asked me "Chewy, who ARE you?"

I continued with relaxed panting and gave him a couple of tail wags. He asked me if I had a connection with God and Jesus. I wagged my tail some more.

Sniffing-checking the fuse

My driver held me as he knelt on the floor and prayed. He prayed for the family and friends of Christopher Adlesperger. He prayed for James Baca and his family. He prayed for all the men and women serving in our military. He thanked God for the blessings given to us during our journey.

TUIALUULUU 23 • KYLE A EGGERS 27
M WARD 25 • TODD C GIBBS 37 • IN C KIM
• CHRISTOPHER S ADLESPERGER 20
C SHIELDS 25 • ROBERT W HOYT 21
BLAZER JR 38 • JASON S CLAIRDAY 21

Portion of the panel in Irvine, California that Chewy wanted to be photographed

The next day, we mounted up after sunrise. Before reaching Amarillo, Texas, we stopped at a large field that had cars planted in the ground. I couldn't figure out why those cars were planted. I sniffed the cars, but my driver and I had questions. Was somebody experimenting to grow new cars? Were the cars brand new when they were planted? Why were they planted? A dog just has to know why hoomans planted these cars.

We stopped at the Harley-Davidson dealership in Amarillo, Texas for an oil change. Like many dealerships, if a rider is travelling and the maintenance supervisor knows it, they do their best to get them on the road as quickly as possible. They allowed me in the dealership since I rode the bike. It was refreshing to take a nap on the cool floor!

We stopped for the night in Tulsa, Oklahoma. We ate at one of my driver's favorite restaurants: What-a-Burger! He loves their jalapeno burgers. They made me a triple hamburger sammich, hold everything but the meat. They threw in an extra hamburger patty. That burger was my appetizer. I had one of my MRE dinners after we checked into the hotel, which was across the interstate from the What-a-Burger.

Before checking out of the hotel in Tulsa, my driver prayed that we would come up on a rider or a group riding to Washington, DC for Rolling Thunder. He asked if God could arrange for them to be Christians. In Cuba, Missouri, we ate lunch at Missouri Hick BBQ on Route 66 – the beef brisket was delicious! My driver and I had our own plates, and I also ate some of his brisket. We sat in the outdoor eating area in the shade, and we talked with lots of hoomans who were interested in me.

Lunch in Cuba, Missouri

On the interstate between Cuba and St. Louis, we passed a lone rider. He had a US flag on the back of his Harley-Davidson Road King. Our cruise control was working and set. As we passed the lone rider, my driver rendered a salute and held it until we passed. The rider took the wingman position behind us through St Louis. East of St Louis, we exited for fuel. The rider followed us to the gas station. We formally met our new friend, Tom Lystrup.

Tail-waggin' happy to have Tom Lystrup with us

Tom was participating in the Run for the Wall, but his Road King broke down in Needles, California. By my calculation, he probably left Needles about the time we should have arrived, but we ended up in Searchlight, Nevada instead.

Tom wasn't sure if he was going to arrive in time for Rolling Thunder. We shared our plan to arrive in DC on Saturday, then participate in the Demonstration on Sunday. Tom started making phone calls to link up with his Run for the Wall platoon. Our prayer for at least one more bike for safety was answered. And, Tom was rejoining his platoon! God is so good to us!

We stayed at a hotel in Indiana, and in West Virginia. In Hurricane, West Virginia, Ali Henley, a friend of my driver, and her family visited at the hotel. Ali and my driver worked together in North Carolina long before I was born. I met Jason (her husband) and their children. It was pawesome being among hooman friends!

Meeting the Henley Children

We're fortunate that Tom was with us. We stopped for lunch about an hour west of DC at Joe's Pizza in Marshall, Virginia. My driver got our bike stuck in the mud on the grass behind the parking lot at Joe's Pizza. Under the thick, green, cool grass, the soil was soft and muddy. Tom helped push us out of the mud and onto the pavement.

At the restaurant, I snoozed near the table while Tom and my driver talked. They are both Christians of different denominations. Talking with Tom gave my driver a perspective that he had not previously known. Perhaps this conversation was part of God's plan for this journey to broaden my driver's understanding of Christianity.

Rolling with Tom through West Virginia

Rolling Thunder was pawesome! We were honored to be the guest of Rolling Thunder Chapter NC1. Ol' Bill "Jammer" found us and introduced us to Bob Bergdahl, the father of SGT Bowe Bergdahl. Bob's wife, Jani, was at another location at the time. Regardless of the circumstances around SGT Bergdahl's captivity, the fact is the Department of Defense categorized SGT Bergdahl as a Prisoner of War. Ol' Bill and I presented Bob with the POW/MIA flag from our Harley-Davidson, and Bob returned it to us and asked us to continue flying the flag until his son returns home. Ol' Bill had the right words for that: Charlie Mike!

We returned home on Memorial Day, stopping at the Harnett County Veterans Memorial in Lillington. We said a prayer and asked God to give us a sign that we did what He wanted us to do. We placed one of my mission dog tags at the memorial marker containing the name "Alvah Denton", my mom's uncle who she never met. We also left one of my mission dog tags at the

Memorial for those who gave their lives during the War on Terror, which includes Fallen Heroes from Iraq and Afghanistan.

While at the Harnett County Veterans Memorial, we were blessed to meet Mr and Mrs Dexter Linear, who were visiting the Memorial to honor those who gave their lives for our freedom. Coincidentally, they know my mom's brother and many hoomans we know. We spent about 20 minutes talking with them.

We rode to the Kipling Cross to thank God for protecting us. To us, the Kipling Cross represented mission completion. Within a couple of minutes of arriving, a black Harley-Davidson Street Glide turned onto the grassy area and rolled towards us. It was Pat Chisenhall, a fellow biker, friend and the pastor of a church in Angier, North Carolina. He told us that he felt the Holy Spirit guiding him to go to the Kipling Cross, so he rode to the Cross. He had no idea that we were just returning from our cross country road trip. Coincidence? What are the chances of Pat and us arriving at about the same time? He felt the Holy Spirit call to him about the time we prayed in Lillington. If we had not spent time with the Linears, we probably would have departed the Cross before Pat arrived. My driver and Pat talked for about 15 minutes. Pat said a prayer for us. Black clouds started moving in and the wind began to pick up. It felt like the Lord was present. We left a mission dog tag at the base of the Kipling Cross, then rode home.

After we arrived home, the bottom fell out of the clouds. According to the Bible, rain is a blessing from God. The first day of our mission started with rain. Our mission ended with rain. We were blessed!

About two weeks later, we attended a flag dedication ceremony by Flags for Fallen Military to honor Jeffrey Webb, Lance Corporal, United States Marine Corps. Jeffrey gave his life while in service to our country. We already knew Jim and Julie Webb, Jeffrey's parents, through the Gold Star Mothers and the USO.

While at the Flags for Fallen Military event, Julie and Jim introduced us to the mother of Sam Griffith, who was a Major in the United States Marine Corps. Sam gave his life while in service to our country. My driver asked me why Sam's name sounded familiar. I looked at him, tilted my head, and gave him a tail wag.

Kipling Cross, Kipling, North Carolina

After we arrived home, my driver had a hunch about Major Griffith. He looked at the photos of names engraved into the pillars in Irvine. Remember those two names that my driver took pictures of but had no idea who these Fallen Heroes were? We just met the other name I sniffed out to my driver in California: Samuel Griffith.

I was upstairs with my driver when he found the photo of Sam's name at the memorial in Irvine. He was speechless. He looked at me, and I looked at him. I gave him tail wags. He got on the floor with me and put his forehead against my forehead. He tried to pray thanks, but he was crying. I just let him hold me. My driver didn't know what to do. He was barkless, but very blessed.

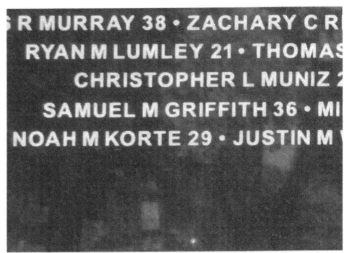

Chewy sniffed Samuel Griffith's name on the panel in Irvine, California

We don't understand why God did these things. Maybe hoomans need to know that their sons and daughters are not forgotten. Maybe God wanted to give us signs that He is with us. Although my driver is a broken man, he loves God and Jesus. Many pawple don't seem to understand why my driver and I do what we do. Sometimes, family members don't seem to understand. My driver admits that he doesn't understand, but he does not turn away from the mission even when others scoff at us.

Chapter 22: Marking my Driver

Most of the events I attend are on my Harley-Davidson, but I attended one dog walk that was three kilometers in downtown Raleigh. The event benefited the SPCA, so hopefully everyone who participated helped save a furry life or two.

I was the only doggie to arrive on a motorcycle. There were hundreds of dogs there, but my arrival drew more attention than we anticipated. We went to the registration table and my driver was given a clip board and pen. He stepped out of the line, and dropped to one knee to complete the paperwork. I wanted my furry friends to know that my driver was mine, so I marked his hip. By the time I finished, the wetness soaked through his jeans, and he jumped up and yelled "Chewy!" I jumped back as if to play, wagging my tail and giving him my happy look of "What?!?!"

My driver's jeans dried during the walk, but everyone thought he stunk. To me, he smelled good.

I enjoyed the walk, but I prefer riding. My bike gets me from point A to point B much faster than my four paws.

Walk? Really?

Chapter 23: Riding for the Kids

Pediatric Brain Tumor Foundation

Over the years, we attended a number of events supporting the Pediatric Brain Tumor Foundation. At my first group ride, I sniffed a brave young boy named Nicholas Weis. He went to Heaven when he was nine years old. He battled brain tumors for seven years. One of his wishes was to have a thousand motorcycles at his Celebration of Life. We had the honor of attending. I would need over a thousand paws to count the number of bikes. It was pawsitively amazing! Bikers have the biggest heart of any group of hoomans.

At the same event that I first met Nicholas, we met a big man with a big heart: Jerry Hart. After Nicholas passed, Jerry continued the mission of raising funds to battle pediatric brain tumors.

One year, my driver and I rode to Tampa, Florida to attend a PBTF event. We thought it would be warm, but the day of the event was one of the coldest days on record in Tampa!

I became a member of Team Brady and attended three events in Asheville, North Carolina. When we prepared to leave for an event one year, it was storming at my house. Hurricane Irene was running up the east coast of North Carolina. Raleigh H.O.G. departed a day or two earlier. They were ahead of the storm. We had tropical storm conditions when we left our house to ride to Asheville. We ran into bands of heavy rain and wind until we were between Greensboro and Winston-Salem, where we had partly cloudy skies, nice temperatures, and breezes.

We rode a scenic route through Diamondback (NC 226A), a portion of the Blue Ridge Parkway and Devil's Staircase (NC 80) on our way to Asheville. The S-curves on NC 80 were fun as my driver pushed my bike left and right several times. We also stopped at the grand opening of Harley-Davidson of Asheville, where we linked up with Steve and Janet Metz and Raleigh H.O.G.

While at the dealership, I let my driver off his leash in a huge field adjacent to the shop. He got away from me and I ran through some mud back to the dealership to find him. I was very muddy! My driver said he was going to give me a bath at the hotel, but Keith Zionts suggested taking me to the bikini bike wash. My driver had baby shampoo in our saddle bag. I turned the bike wash into a bikini biker-dog wash.

Why did we ride to Asheville through a storm? At the time, Brady was five years old and battling a brain tumor. He couldn't attend the event the previous year because he was undergoing chemotherapy or something. My driver promised to have me at the event if Brady was going to be there. We kept our promise. The storm didn't stop us.

On Sunday morning of the event, we linked up with Raleigh H.O.G. again and with Statesville H.O.G. south of Asheville. Keith Zionts led Team Brady on a ride to Biltmore Square Mall, the starting point for the event. We don't know how many bikes were there, but we know it was a few hundred. The police-escorted ride took us on a section of the Blue Ridge Parkway and then on a highway to Lake Lure. It was a pawruffic day to put my tongue in the wind! At Lake Lure, lunch was served for the Celebration of Life. One of the riders didn't like her sandwich, so she gave it to me. It was a turkey sammich and I loved it! Team Brady placed in the top five in fund raising and we had our pictures taken with the Stars – the children are referred to as Stars. After the Celebration of Life, we rode with Raleigh H.O.G. back to Raleigh led by Steve Metz.

The Miracle League Ride

One day, I attended four events in one day, including one for kids! I was a pooped pup that evening. We started the day meeting the Golden Retrievers from Patriot Rovers at the Ride for the Rovers. There were six Rovers there. Patriot Rovers rescues Golden Retrievers, trains them, and assigns them as service dogs to wounded warriors or veterans battling Post-Traumatic Stress Disorder (PTSD). Each Rover is named after a Fallen Hero. The Patriot Rovers was founded by David Cantara. David sometimes refers to me as the "original Patriot Rover". We were told that part of the idea for the Patriot Rovers comes from my background of being rescued and bringing comfort to my driver.

After the Ride for the Rovers rolled out of Ray Price Harley-Davidson, my driver attended the wedding of John Headrick and Hannah Stallings inside the showroom of Ray Price Harley-Davidson. I stayed outside with Dave, the General Manager of Ray Price H-D.

After the wedding, my driver and I mounted up for the annual Miracle League Ride. I first heard of the Miracle League through Allison Shackelford. Each year, Allison and Kim Butler looked after me and introduced me to lots of little pawple. The Miracle League is a baseball league for children with special needs. Cary Police Department ensured we arrived safely at the ball field at an elementary school in Cary, NC.

The bikers put smiles on the children's faces. I did my part to help. My nose always finds the burger and hot dog stand, but my driver tells me to sniff in another direction.

After our pipes had time to cool, we let kids mount my Harley-Davidson for pictures. I'm gentle around kids and some just hug me because I'm soft like a teddy bear. It brings the kids and their families a moment of joy or a brief smile to their faces. Life is tough – tougher for some than for others. These kids and their parents have the courage to face every challenge and overcome them. We admire their strength and courage!

Give Kids the World

Paula Schronce asked me to attend a "Give Kids the World" event in Fayetteville – and to bring my driver, too. We didn't participate in the ride because there were lots of activities available while the bikers were out riding. I met lots of new friends and let some of them mount my driver's seat on my Harley-Davidson for photos with me. The smiles from the children and their parents were worth it. The kids were great in not touching all the buttons and switches on my bike. We can handle sticky finger smudges on the gas tank. Sometimes, I'll lick hands and fingers before they mount my bike.

Lots and lots of gift packages were raffled and there were lots of organizations there. We were at the event for about four hours mingling, rubbing with old friends, and meeting new friends. According to their website, Give Kids the World is a non-profit organization that fulfills the wishes of children with life-threatening illnesses and their families to have a memorable, cost-free visit to attractions in Central Florida and Give Kids the World Village.

Month of the Military Child

Every month has several themes. One of the themes for April is Month of the Military Child. I was honored to ride with the Patriot Guard Riders for several annual events to attend flag raising ceremonies at Butner Elementary School on Ft Bragg. When we arrived, many of us revved our engines and blasted our horns. The kids cheered and clapped! Many thanks to Ft Bragg Military Police in escorting us to the school and ensuring we arrived safely. I had a pawruffic time seeing Principal Joiner each year and meeting other teachers and students. I was in a few group photos and when we were leaving the school, I wandered into two classrooms to sniff-ello (sniff them hello) the kids.

I wonder why some hoomans call the children "brats," such as Army brat, military brat, etc. Brat has at least two meanings. One meaning is that of a spoiled or ill-mannered child. The other meaning is the child of a military service member. I'm barking about the child of military service members, because, in my doggy opawnion and generally barking, children of our service members have challenges that many children don't have, like having to move every couple of years, having your dad or mom deploy to defend us, a parent being at sea for a very long time, a parent being assigned to a place where the family can't go, and many more challenges.

Even routine training can be dangerous. My mom remembers the first time in which my driver was injured during a night airborne training exercise. For my civilian friends, airborne soldiers are the paratroopers who jump from perfectly good planes in full combat gear. My mom received a call at o'dark thirty and the first thing the Sergeant Major said was something like "Mrs. Ewing, your husband's alive. He gave me an order to not tell you anything and to just tell you he's running late. So, he's running late." My mom knew to go to Womack Army Hospital.

What does being a military brat mean to my driver and my mom? It means one or both of the child's parents are willing to sacrifice their lives for our country. That fact makes the children of our service members very, very special. I bark the same thing for children of law enforcement officers and firefighters – not all of them may be putting their lives on the line for our country, but they are certainly risking their lives for the communities they serve. Seeing how only about seven percent of Americans serve our country through the Armed Forces, I wonder how many hoomans really and truly understand the sacrifices from each child and their families.

Former Defense Secretary Casper Weinberger may have declared April as the Month of the Military Child, but we should honor our military families every day. It's not just the service member making sacrifices – it's the spouses, children and even the fur-kids!

When you say your prayers, please include the children of our military service members, and especially the children and families of those who gave the ultimate sacrifice while in service to our country.

Chewy was around children at home; pictured with one of Chewy's hooman nieces

Chapter 24: Helping Veterans

Tyler Jeffries

Have you ever met a Wounded Warrior? If you have, did you notice that all are very humble, especially when you call them a Hero? Tyler Jeffries is among those humble American Heroes.

When we met Tyler, he was a Specialist in the US Army. He deployed to Afghanistan. According to the Salisbury Post, Tyler's team was completing a mission to clear explosives in a deserted village. Tyler lost both of his legs to a non-detectable, command wired Improvised Explosive Device.

Tyler eventually arrived at Walter Reed National Military Medical Center in Bethesda, Maryland. Why did Tyler interest us? Tyler was with the 2nd Infantry Division when he was wounded. My driver was serving in the 2nd Infantry Division in Korea at about the time that Tyler was born.

Since my driver recently had a procedure done to his neck (which resulted from when he and I were hit), he prayed for strength to be able to endure a full day in the saddle. Thomas Sanders, my driver and I rode up to the DC area on a very cold day a few days before Christmas. It was so cold that we rolled through snow flurries while on the George Washington Parkway north of Arlington! Hmmmm. Why does it seem like I ride through snow when I'm with Thomas and my driver?

Tyler was cleared to depart Walter Reed on leave to visit his family in Concord, North Carolina. The temperature was in the teens when we departed the hotel in Maryland. Five motorcycles led by Dennis Markle departed Walter Reed at o'dark thirty to escort Tyler and his family nearly 390 miles to Concord. It was c-c-c-c-old!

We rode south on I-95. At a rest area south of the DC metropolitan area, we rolled into a rest area. About a dozen bikes were waiting for us. We did a roll-by and the group joined us.

Near Richmond, we rolled into a gas station, where about another dozen bikes joined us. It was a pre-planned fuel stop. Dennis coordinated the link-ups very well.

By the time we reached the border of Virginia and North Carolina, the group had grown to about 30 motorcycles. The Virginia Patriot Guard handed off to North Carolina Patriot Guard at the first North Carolina rest area on I-85. Sheriff Deputies from Cabarrus and Iredell Counties were with the Patriot Guard to ensure a safe escort. Most of the Virginia bikers returned home, but a few, including Dennis Markle and Philip Mahoney, rode the entire distance to Concord.

While at the North Carolina rest area, Tyler must have mentioned wanting to ride. There was a delay and I noticed hoomans getting an extra jacket, insulated pants, a helmet and a head/neck cover. Tyler rode! Thomas became Tyler's driver for 120 miles to Greensboro. That was totally pawesome! NEVER tell a wounded warrior that he or she won't be able to do something!

North of Henderson, a large crowd was standing on the overpass. They waved as Tyler and his escort rumbled under them. From that point, several overpasses had firefighters, law enforcement officers and patriotic Americans standing on them to welcome Tyler home.

Near Butner, our LEO (Law Enforcement Officer) escort coordinated a rolling merge of more Patriot Guard Riders. When we arrived in Greensboro for refuel, a news reporter was waiting. There were many more bikers standing by to join the escort. On the final leg from Greensboro to Concord, LEO coordinated two more rolling merges.

By the time we reached Concord, news reporters estimated several hundred bikes and lots of cars. Hoomans were lined on the streets with flags, banners and signs to welcome Tyler home. We arrived at Cross Pointe Church in Concord late in the afternoon. Tyler asked everyone to keep our military men and women in our prayers. When the focus was on Tyler, he wanted us to focus on all those serving in the military. That says something about this humble, brave, young man!

During the trip, I wore a bandana with the 2ID patch. Before Thomas, my driver and I headed home, we gave that bandana to Tyler as a reminder that there are a handful of Americans who are willing to take time out of their schedule to show their respect and love. These hoomans put words into action!

My driver and I began assembling photos and videos to create a music video to memorialize this event for Tyler. To add to the pawesome event, Mike Corrado (a singer/songwriter who is also a Marine) gave us permission to use his song "Still in the Fight" for the video honoring Tyler.

JB Kerns

At another event, Fuzzy and Gail Melton invited us to an event to support a Wounded Warrior: Corporal JB Kerns (USMC) of Ararat, Virginia. JB was on his third tour as a combat engineer when his vehicle was destroyed by an IED. JB sacrificed both of his legs and an arm for our country. We couldn't attend the event in the prior year, but we were told that there was a benefit concert starring Gary Sinise and the Lieutenant Dan Band.

At this event, there was a fellowship of hoomans gathering to continue the efforts of raising funds to build JB a smart home under the "Building for America's Bravest" program. The ride, sponsored by Marine Corps League Detachment 908 with support from Rolling Thunder's chapter from Johnson City, Tennessee, began at the National Guard Armory in Martinsville, Virginia and ended at Dan River Park in Ararat.

The weather forecast was for rain. Before leaving our house, I put my paws together and prayed with my driver for the rain to hold until after the event. We rode with Thomas Sanders, Jim and Christina Kazakavage, and Rudy Hendrix from Sanford, North Carolina to Martinsville. God gave us beautiful weather, but I reckon we should have prayed for good weather until we returned home because we rode through heavy rain in Winston-Salem. (I still didn't see "Raining Cats and Dogs")

Fuzzy led the group and Law Enforcement Officers ensured our safety from Martinsville to Ararat. The motorcycles were split into two groups with cages led by JB between the groups. The route was scenic with sweeps and curves.

Local businesses provided door prizes. There were soooo many door prizes that every participant received one! I won six Slim Jims – the perfect door prize for a furry little guy like me. The businesses were very considerate in providing thoughtful door prizes that could be carried home by a biker.

After the post-ride activities at Dan River Park, our group decided to ride Squirrel Spur Road from Ararat to the Blue Ridge Parkway before heading home. It was a fun road with a few twisties and curves – and a funny name!

I'm grateful to Ray Price Harley-Davidson for taking care of my bike in time for this event in Martinsville. We were on our third transmission and it took a few weeks for the re-engineered transmission to arrive. But, once it arrived at RPHD, they had her ready for the road quickly.

Chapter 25: Officer Down and Granny Down

Most of the time, my driver and I refer to "Fallen Heroes" as those who lost their lives while serving our country. One day in early summer, we rode with lots of friends in support of another group of Fallen Heroes – law enforcement officers who gave their lives in the line of duty. I think these events are sometimes called "Officer Down" memorial events. This specific event was sponsored by Blue Knights. The reason we knew about it is because we read that Mike Brown (a veteran, law enforcement officer, and biker friend) was leading the event.

My driver and I planned to go to Ft Belvoir, Virginia to spend time with warriors at a barbecue. The forecast was for a hot and humid day, with showers between our home and Virginia. About 10 minutes after the leaving our house, we ran into heavy rain. My driver had a feeling that maybe God didn't want us to go to Ft Belvoir. My driver decided to change course to Fayetteville to attend the Officer Down event. We had hopes that the rain would be scattered.

Arriving in the rain

When we arrived in Fayetteville, my driver was soaked. There were about 50 bikes ready to roll. With law enforcement escort the entire route, we rode to Jones Lake State Park near Elizabethtown, then back to Fayetteville for BBQ where my driver and I shared fried chicken, pulled pork and "moosh balls" (that's what my driver calls hush puppies). We had scattered rain during the ride, but by the time the group returned to Fayetteville, most of the rain had moved out.

Officer Down Memorial, Fayetteville, North Carolina

On our way home, we stopped for fuel and a person asked us what we do when it rains. My driver looked at him, said "Get wet" and grinned.

God must have planned to divert us to Fayetteville instead of riding to Virginia. Soon after we returned home, my mom called my hooman granny (my mom's mom) and she didn't sound right. My driver and my mom rushed to her house, which is about three minutes from our house. My granny didn't want to go to the hospital, so my driver told her she had a choice: my driver would carry her to the truck and take her to the hospital, or they would call 911 for an ambulance. My granny said she wasn't going anywhere and my mom was already dialing 911. My hooman granny had a stroke in her brain stem. She went peacefully to Heaven a few days later.

If my driver and I had gone to Virginia, he would not have been home to help my mom with my granny. Coincidence? My driver told me many times that there are too many of these kinds of things happening to be simply coincidences. He said that God is leading us and we just need to pray and pay attention the best we can. My driver and I tried as hard as we could to understand what God wants my driver and me to do.

My granny is a solid Christian. My pawrents know that their faith in God and His Son will allow them to see my granny again. Do dogs go to Heaven? I certainly hope so 'cuz I'd love to spend eternity with my family and all my Christian friends.

Tongue in the Wind

Chapter 26: A Flight and a Ferry

I'm not sure if I'm barking this correctly, but why is it that when organizations need money, they go to bikers and ask them to pay to ride?   How many organizations do you know go to car drivers and ask them to pay to drive? Why do bikers do it? In my opawnion, it's because, as a percentage, a larger portion of bikers (as compared to the non-biker population) have big hearts and they give their time and money to great causes or to help another member of the biker family.   Perhaps bikers are in an informal brotherhood and sisterhood to unite and help others.

While my driver was unemployed, we had to choose between gas money or pay to ride in an event. Our priority went to "no-fee" missions to honor our Fallen Heroes, military and veterans. A few organizations respected our priority. My driver was asked to bring me to an event and ride as their guest.   Sometimes, an anonymous person or group paid the ride fee so that we could participate and do our usual thing of taking photos to document the event. The occasional times when someone anonymously covered our ride fee speaks to the big hearts of the biker family. To all – we humbly and respectfully thank you.

One year, we started our own set of rides, which we called Remembrance Rides.   It sort-of, kind-of stems from our rides across the USA.   The purpose was to Honor and Remember our Fallen Heroes, those serving now, and our veterans. There were no fees, no donations and no registration. It was open to bikers and cagers. They simply linked-up with us and rode for the entire trip, or for part of it.

Our first Remembrance Ride was from Sanford to Little Switzerland on the Blue Ridge Parkway.   The route to Little Switzerland took us on a segment of road nicknamed "Back of the Diamond" or "Diamondback". Since this ride was intended as a loooong day trip, the ride to Diamondback was mostly interstate.

Ride participants included Tod and Kendra Hartwick, Jim and Christina Kazakavage, Darryn Mewhorter, Snoopy (and his driver, Tim Wall), Thomas Sanders, and Mark and Jasmine Russell with their retired Military Working Dog, Brit. Richard Chowning rode up from Charlotte. He met us near Morganton, where we stopped for fuel and lunch. Richard rode with us to Little Switzerland and to Boone.

Stuck in traffic – all lanes had to exit due to construction

Little Switzerland is at the top of Diamondback. We stopped at a store in Little Switzerland. While some of the riders went inside the store, some stayed outside with me. A dog came to visit me, but he wasn't very nice. I was wagging my tail and expecting a friendly greeting. Instead, that dog didn't seem to like me and he started a fight. My driver broke us up, and the store owner came out to tell the dog to go home. I was bleeding and the store owner apologized while Christi and my driver checked me. I reckon not all dogs are friendly like me.

Before leaving, I met a nice lady with the road name "The BROAD". I reckon she was like my driver and me – taking time to ramble around the country. We learned a few months later that a driver in a vehicle hit her and she lost one of her legs. We followed her on social media and were impressed with her emotional and physical strength. She got back in the saddle.

After Little Switzerland, we rode the Blue Ridge Parkway to Boone. On the Blue Ridge Parkway, we stopped at a couple of overlooks. It was beautiful with temperatures nearly perfect with low humidity. Riding downhill from Boone, we could feel the humidity starting to rise. Richard headed south back to Charlotte.

Visiting Little Switzerland, North Carolina

We stopped for fuel and quick dinner south of Mount Airy ("Mayberry"). We saw rain in the distance, and we put on our rain suits. Me? I just tuck in behind my driver to stay dry. Before we reached Winston-Salem, we rolled into a down pour. It was raining so hard, we missed the exit because we couldn't see it. We took the next exit and parked the bikes under cover at a gas pump. My driver cleaned his glasses and attached a face shield to his helmet. After a few minutes, the rain slowed down. By the time we got on the right road, the rain stopped. We returned home way after dark and didn't roll through any more rain after Winston-Salem. It was a loooong day, and my driver and I had a snoring contest during the night.

A few months later, we held our second Remembrance Ride. It was just as pawesome as the first! We rode to Oak Island to fly in a bi-plane piloted by Jim Banky. Jim and Laura own and operate Suncoast Aviation at the Cape Fear Regional Jetport.

We linked up with Gold Star Mom and Dad Jim and Christi, Snoopy and his driver, and Thomas Sanders in Benson. From there, we rolled on the interstate towards Wilmington, then to Oak Island.

Riding the Blue Ridge Parkway

At the airport, there were about 20 hoomans waiting for us, including my mom and my hooman brother (Keith) and his family (wife Christine and daughter Lillie). We had posted about our destination in social media, and I didn't realize I had friends at the coast.

Jim and Christi were on the first flight. They carried onto the aircraft my driver's military helmet flight bag that had a Gold Star Roster inside – one of the rosters that we carried on our last cross-country ride. The bag also contained the last few dog tags from that ride across the USA as well as bandanas such as a NATO Canada bandana (a gift from Gerry Corbin and the UN/NATO Canada Veterans), my bandana from the Combat Veterans Motorcycle Association NC 15-1, and two Psalm 91 bandanas that were blessed in Israel and given to me by Donna Taylor. Among over 5,000 heroes in that roster was Jim and Christi's son: Adam K. Ginett.

My driver and I flew in the second sortie, followed by Snoopy and his driver, then my pawrent's son and his wife, Keith and Christine.

Snoopy and I had the same reaction: we perked up when the 7-cylinder radial engine fired up and when Jim throttled up for take-off. To us, it was windier and louder, but just as cool as riding on a bike. I pawthored a short picture story called "A Flight and a Ferry" based on that day and posted it on my social media fan page and my website.

Snoopy and I are waiting patiently to fly

In the cockpit

After our flights, we rode to Southport and ate at the outdoor seating area of a well-known seafood restaurant. Snoopy and I met lots of new friends.

After the meal, we rode to the ferry port, and crossed the water to Fort Fisher. It was a smooth, breezy ferry ride. Snoopy and I didn't want to dismount, so we chilled on the bikes. Between meeting new friends, we tried to nap a little.

After we disembarked from the ferry, we rolled through Wilmington and towards home into the night

Meeting new friends on the ferry

Chapter 27: The Greatest Shepherd

Sometimes, my driver and I are asked to bark our testimony at a church or at a meeting. My driver tells stories that tend to make other hoomans laugh. I think hoomans enjoy hearing stories about me and my adventures, including an explanation of the "slobber factor".

At one church service, my driver said something that touched a few dog lovers. Our last name is Ewing, which is Scottish and my driver thinks is linked to ewes (sheep). When he was a teenager, his family had a border collie. Before me, my driver adopted a Sheltie. He likes us herding dogs because of our smarts. But, then he said something during that service that made sense to a few hoomans ... maybe Jesus, the greatest Shepherd in the Universe, put herding dogs in my driver's life to guide him – to take direction from Jesus to herd him to a specific place. Maybe Jesus put herding dogs in other hooman's lives to guide them, too.

Hoomans might not forgive other hoomans for doing wrong, but God will. When my driver accepted Jesus as his Lord and Savior, God forgave my driver for his wrongdoings. He will forgive you, too! All you have to do is ask God for His forgiveness, and accept His Son, Jesus, as the only way to spend eternity with God.

I don't know if dogs go to Heaven, but my driver and I pray a lot that we can spend eternity together with God and Jesus in Heaven.

Tongue in the Wind

Chapter 28: Charlie Mike III

Combat Veterans Motorcycle Association NC 15-1 held Charlie Mike III in mid-summer. I was about 10 years old in hooman years. Like previous Charlie Mikes, the mission was to ride 1,000 miles in 24 hours. This mission honored those who served in World War II. Charlie Mike is phonetic for the letters CM, which means "continue the mission".

CMIII started at the Harnett County Veterans Memorial in Lillington. We rode to the aircraft carrier USS Yorktown (Charleston, South Carolina), battleship USS North Carolina (Wilmington, North Carolina), battleship USS Wisconsin (Norfolk, Virginia), a section of the WWII Memorial Highway in Richmond, and ended at the Airborne Special Operations Museum in Fayetteville. Like previous Charlie Mikes, the CVMA chapter submitted all of the documentation to the IronButt Association on behalf of the riders.

Enroute to Charleston, South Carolina

It was humid, but as long as we were rolling, it felt OK to me. We left Lillington around mid-morning. We had fuel stops every 100 miles. Everyone was reminded to reset their trip odometer at each fuel stop. If anyone got separated from the group, they knew to ride the route until they reached 100 miles since the last fuel stop, then continue on the route to the next gas station, or the next exit if on the interstate.

We arrived at the USS Yorktown at about mid-afternoon. After leaving the aircraft carrier, we were in a lot of stop-n-go traffic.

Charlie Mike III Riders at USS Yorktown

In Georgetown, we encountered some careless hoomans in cars. Jim and Christi (their second Charlie Mike) were nearly taken out by a car as we turned into a gas station. Leaving the gas station, Wizard, Schmuck, my driver and I were nearly taken out by a lady driving a blue SUV. We were on a four lane road and she was drifting among the lanes. My driver and I caught up with her. We stayed slightly behind her SUV and in the left lane for about 15 seconds. We watched her with her head down the entire time while she was texting. Whisky Tango Bravo, Over. (What the bark?) My driver yelled to me that he hopes she gets pulled over. We accelerated to pass her and get clear of her. About a minute later, we saw blue lights in our rear view mirror. My driver muttered some words that I couldn't hear. The blue SUV pulled over with the law enforcement officer. She was caught!

Goofing around in the saddle north of Myrtle Beach, South Carolina

Charlie Mike III Riders at USS North Carolina

Mike "Krzywuf" Wilson drove from Lillington to US-17 near Ocean Isle to intercept us and take pictures and video as we rode north on US-17. We arrived at the USS North Carolina at about dusk. We stopped for a few photos, then rode to Goldsboro.

Enroute to Goldsboro, my driver's neck and left shoulder was hurting. He was still struggling from when he and I were hit a few years back. He thought about aborting when we arrived in Goldsboro, but we were carrying a special flag for Ed

"TailGunner" Williams, who went to be with our Lord earlier in the year. Ed rode in Charlie Mike II, but his bike had an electrical problem and could not finish the ride.

We arrived in Goldsboro about an hour after dark. We had a few extra minutes for a quick dinner. Although my driver was in pain, he decided to "continue our mission". Being a former soldier, he endured much more and knows that our men and women in uniform are enduring more than my driver's muscle and nerve pain.

CVMA VA 27 met us east of Emporia, Virginia and led us to the USS Wisconsin in Norfolk, arriving about two hours after midnight. It was awesome that biker brothers met us to lead us to our waypoint destination. We dismounted for about 30 minutes, took a group photo, and stretched our legs.

Sleepy, but awake, in Norfolk, Virginia. (Notice my helmet hair?)

While enroute from Norfolk to Richmond, my driver had a glimpse of an object flying by the right side of his head. It happened so quickly that he didn't have time to react or get a good view of the object or critter. When we refueled in Richmond, we noticed that our Honor and Remember flag was gone. We think the object hit our center flag and snapped our flag pole at the base.

Wizard told us he saw something slide by him on the pavement, but didn't know what it was at the time. Sadly, that Honor and Remember flag was to be presented to the Dogwood Chapter of the American Gold Star Mothers. That flag was on two rides across the USA in honor of Fallen Heroes and it was on its second Charlie Mike. The missing flag was kind of a reminder of how quickly someone can be taken from us.

In Richmond, we stopped at a gas station. The lights and pumps were on for credit card purchases, but the store was closed. The restrooms for hoomans were inside the store. While we were refueling, the ladies were walking into the dark areas behind the bushes. I was curious. I stood and looked in the direction. I was ready to let my driver know if something seemed suspicious. They all returned safely. One of the ladies took me to the grassy area so I could empty my bladder. She brought me back to my driver at about the time my driver fired up the bike to move it out of the way from the gas pump.

My driver connected the leash to the bike, and he walked towards bushes. When I couldn't see him anymore, I pulled on the leash and started barking loudly. A few seconds later, my driver stepped out from the bushes. Friends were laughing. My driver said "Thanks for blowing my cover, Chewy!" I was soooo happy to see my driver. I don't understand why he was embarrassed.

We mounted up, departed the gas station, and about 30 minutes later, we arrived at another gas station that was open. My driver called that time of the morning "EMNT" (Early Morning Nautical Twilight). It's the time in the morning when the sky starts to get a little light in the eastern horizon. We dismounted for about 30 minutes.

At the gas station, there was a lady who seemed a little drunk. Well, maybe not drunk, but she was acting strangely for a hooman. She insisted Wizard give her a ride on his bike. She sprayed some smelly perfume stuff on Mike's bike. Hoomans might think it smelled good, but it made me sneeze. I don't think any of us understood the reason she sprayed Mike's bike. When Wizard walked into the store, the lady came over to me and petted me until Wizard returned to his bike. Then, she started asking Wizard for a ride again. Most of us were laughing about it when she told

"Weeeeeeeeeeeeezard" to give her a ride. The lady gave up and walked to the hotel next to the gas station. My driver felt the lady was "lost." I lay next to him while he knelt and said a silent prayer for her to turn to God and for God to help guide her. The group mounted up, fired up the steal horses, and continued our southbound journey.

After crossing into North Carolina, other CVMA bikers and friends linked up with us along the way. We arrived at the Airborne Special Operations Museum in Fayetteville at about mid-morning. We rode about 1,060 miles within 24 hours. This specific mission was successfully completed – both from a Charlie Mike perspective and an IronButt perspective.

Three-time Charlie Mike Riders
l-r: William "QuietMan" Holman, Brian Volk, my driver, Tim "Wizard" Prescott, me (sitting)

There were four bikers and a pawsenger who completed this Charlie Mike and the two previous Charlie Mikes: QuietMan, Wizard, Brian Volk, my driver and me (the pawsenger).

We rode about an hour to get to the Kipling Cross. After spending time at the Cross thanking God for watching over all of us and asking Him to protect our military service members, we headed home. My driver gave me a cool, refreshing bath before he took a shower. We slept on the living room floor until it was supper time. My mom said that we both snored loudly. Sometimes, my driver and I alternated snoring, then snored together. She was amused and glad it wasn't night time.

Tongue in the Wind

Chapter 29: Helmet on the Ground

We were planning to attend a Flags for Fallen Military ceremony. We went to the address that was posted earlier in the week. Although the location was in Cameron, North Carolina, the map software identified the address as being in Carthage. So, Carthage is where we went. We arrived early at the staging location, which was an auto parts store. By staging time, no one was there and we figured we weren't at the right place. Since the location was Cameron, we backtracked to Cameron and didn't see an auto parts store.

Since the mission start time already passed, I decided to take my driver home the loooong way. When we rolled onto NC-87 and started heading towards Spring Lake, we saw blue lights in the median. We noticed Thomas Sanders and his white truck, so we rode on until we could safely turn around. After we turned around, we stopped on the inside shoulder. We saw Thomas, asked if he was OK, he gave us a thumbs up and pointed to the side of his truck. From what we saw, it looked like the van parked in front of him side-swiped Thomas' truck. We headed home, but since we were pointed back towards Sanford, we decided to take NC-27, which is all two-lanes.

On NC-27, we were heading up a slight hill. Over the hill coming towards us was a white mustang pulling out from behind a gray pickup to pass. He was headed right at us! It was a no-passing zone (double yellow lines). My driver hit the brakes. I was pushed into my driver's back. I don't know how he did it, but he threw the bike to the right without laying it down. He put the bike between the white line and the grass. There were only a few inches to about a foot of pavement there. He stayed on the pavement while the mustang stayed in our lane heading towards us. I think the pickup hit his brakes before they got to us. The mustang stayed in our lane rolling right at us. He missed hitting us by a few inches! It looked like his side mirrors may have passed under our mirrors. That was too close! He must have been travelling at 70-80 mph!

My driver rolled the bike onto the grass. I could hear him say "Thank you, Lord! Thank you, Lord! Thank you, Lord!" He said it so many times that I didn't have enough paws to count that many times.

After he stopped the bike, my driver turned around in the saddle and he asked me, he says, "Chew-Chew, are you alright?" I leaned forward to give him a lick under the chin and my driver lost his balance and dropped my Harley! Can you believe that? He throws the bike around on the pavement, and he drops it when we're stopped.

He unbuckled me from my seat, and I watched him try to get the bike up. I watched him and I said to him, I said, "Why iz you trying to lift the saddle with your butt?"□

He took his helmet off and put it on the road's shoulder behind the bike. He went back to trying to get the bike back up. He scrunched his big ol' butt under the side of the saddle and was grunting loudly. At first, I thought maybe he was passing gas, then I thought maybe he wanted to play so I came to him with my tail wagging.

A few bikers rolled by, but no one stopped. Doesn't the helmet on the ground mean anything anymore? Is that old-school stuff that no one knows?

My driver finally got the bike upright, but he killed his back and his hips. He cranked it up, put it in gear, and moved it to the edge of the pavement. He was hurting and didn't want to lift me to my seat. He told me it was OK to hop on the bike, so I did and got into my saddle. We rolled home.

We got a short look at the mustang driver, but he was moving so fast. My driver was trying to keep control of the bike and he didn't think to try to get the license number. He was moving so fast that my driver probably wouldn't be able to read the license. He was a young man with dark hair. Maybe a teenager in a hurry? Regardless, that kid almost made my mom a widow and furchildless.

The driver in the pick-up didn't stop either. Maybe he saw that there was no collision.

On the way home, my driver and I thought about how close we came to getting hit again. It seems like God gave us a purpawse to be here. What if we were hit? I'm not pawsitively sure where doggies go when they die, because there is nothing in The Bible about dogs going to Heaven. The Bible was written for hoomans, so there is nothing in there about what happens to doggies when they die. The Bible mentions animals in Heaven, so I have hope that I will go to Heaven.

My driver knows he will be going to Heaven. How does he know? Because Jesus is his Lord and Savior. Jesus is also my mom's Lord and Savior. We've been to lots and lots of funerals over the years, and we've heard hoomans say things like "He was a good person, so he's in Heaven" or "We know he's in Heaven because he died for his country". There's only one road to Heaven, and that's with Jesus. Being a good person and dying for your country, family and friends is honorable, but that's not the path to Heaven. The Bible states that the only way to Heaven is by accepting God's Son, Jesus, as your Lord and Savior. If you're not absolutely certain that you are going to Heaven when you die, talk to a pastor at a Bible-based church. You never know when someone is going to pull out in front of you.

As for the helmet on the ground, that is a distress signal. When a biker places her/his helmet on the ground behind the bike, please stop to help. If you don't own a bike, you might impress the biker with your knowledge of that S-O-S signal. If the biker asks where you learned that signal, just tell 'em that a biker dog taught you a new trick.

Tongue in the Wind

Chapter 30: Ride Across the USA 2014

Months before our third cross-country mission, we began updating the Fallen Heroes Roster. We searched for names of military service members who passed while on active duty, but not in combat. We searched for those killed while training, passed from a medical condition, killed in a vehicle crash, etc. As we approached our mission date, we began printing two copies of the Roster: one for Craig Hardy and one for us.

Our plan was to ride up to West Virginia, then ride west towards Denver. In Colorado, we planned to visit Chris "Gundy" Gunderson at the national cemetery. We were hoping to link-up with Gundy's wife at the cemetery, Myrtle "Peaches". From Denver, the plan was to ride to the Iraq/Afghanistan War Memorial in Irvine, California. The plan was to take the southern route on our eastward journey, stop in North Carolina, then link-up with Rolling Thunder NC-1 to attend Rolling Thunder in Washington, DC over the Memorial Day weekend. That was the plan.

On the morning of the start of our adventure, Craig linked up with us in Sanford. We rode to a fast food restaurant, where we ate a quick breakfast in the parking lot with Angi (Craig's wife) and their grandson. Angi and my mom share something in common – they both battled cancer and survived!

We rode northwest towards West Virginia. We rode by "Mount Pilot" (Pilot Mountain) and we stopped for lunch south of "Mayberry" (Mount Airy, North Carolina). We met a Marine veteran and his newborn son. We talked for a while and the veteran wanted to take pictures of his son with me. I mounted my Harley-Davidson and posed with the young baby.

The weather was pawfect until we reached Virginia. Craig and my driver put on their rain suits. Me? I stay dry by tucking in behind my driver. In West Virginia, we ran into more rain, most of it seemed heavy. We took a short detour to check out the New River Gorge Bridge, but it was too foggy and rainy to get a clear view of it.

Craig Hardy with Pilot Mountain in the background

Soon after leaving the bridge, we had problems. We could hear loud grinding coming from the area of my driver's feet. The bike started lurching. The engine seemed to be running OK. We exited and pulled over. My Harley-Davidson wouldn't go any further. My driver first thought it was the primary drive. Since we only heard the noise when releasing the clutch, he thought it may be the transmission. Since my Harley-Davidson is on its third gear pack, that seemed to make sense. Craig and my driver are H.O.G. members. The first lesson learned is to put your H.O.G. card where you can find it. Why? H.O.G. members participate in a roadside assistance program. My driver knew our H.O.G. card was in one of the bags. Craig had his card in his wallet.

My driver talked with the H.O.G. representative on the phone. We learned there was a Harley-Davidson dealership about two miles from us. My driver called the dealership. It was mid-afternoon. The dealership was closing in 30 minutes and did not want to help us or fetch us. The person he talked with on the phone also told him that their service department was closed on Sundays and Mondays, so they wouldn't be able to look at it until Tuesday or later, if we could get it to their dealership on Tuesday.

My driver was not a happy hooman, mostly because he felt the dealership was knowingly stranding us on the side of the road. My driver called the H.O.G. service again. They arranged for a recovery vehicle to get the bike and to arrange a hotel for the night. Those H.O.G. hoomans are pawesome!

While waiting, the rain gradually stopped. We were stranded on the side of the road for over two hours before J&J towing arrived, took us to a hotel about 25 miles away in Summerville, and took my Harley-Davidson to their shop for safekeeping. We checked in with our loved ones by phone. It was looking like our mission ended.

Wet and broken down on the side of the road

Craig and my driver talked in the hotel. Both were disappointed. My driver suggested that Craig take the funeral flag, dog tags and continue the mission to California – Charlie Mike! Craig wanted to ensure we remained OK and offered to stay with us. How do you convince a veteran to leave another veteran behind?

My driver and I narrowed our choices to two options: (1) find a way to bring my bike to Ray Price Harley-Davidson in Raleigh, or (2) pay J&J towing to take the bike to the nearest dealership, which would not be able to work on it until Tuesday. My driver searched on the internet for resources. He found a rental car place and a truck rental place. The question was whether or not they would be open on Sunday. If the rental car place was open, the plan was to return home, fetch our pick-up truck, and take the bike to Ray Price. If we found a small rental truck, we would load the bike and go. Pawsonally, I was OK with either scenario. Our problem would be resolved over time, and I was enjoying being with my driver.

Craig was unsure about going on to California and leaving us behind. My driver and I decided to figure out a way to get the bike to Ray Price. We did not know the problem with bike, so we were unsure how long the bike would be in the shop. Since the bike was in J&J's garage, we couldn't inspect it. My driver and I convinced Craig that we were safe. We just needed to find a rental car or truck. The worst case scenario is that we would be in the hotel until Monday.

The next morning, the weather was pawfect! It was sunny and the morning was chilly. We ate breakfast at a gas station next to the hotel. There was a fast food area that prepared breakfast. During breakfast, Craig and my driver talked over the plans of Craig continuing the mission, and my driver and I would evacuate the casualty (our bike) to the rear. I listened. It sounded good to me!

After we returned to the hotel, we gave Craig the 200 dog tags we were carrying and the funeral flag. Craig hugged my driver and me, he mounted up, and he headed west on his adventure and mission. I sensed my driver was sad that we could not follow. It felt odd watching Craig roll away. I sensed my driver's determination to transport our bike to Raleigh.

During our previous cross-country rides, our contingency plan was to put the bike in a rental truck and bring her home if we could not get her repaired in a day or two. In West Virginia, the service departments are closed on Sundays and Mondays (or so we were told by H.O.G.). It was the right decision to try to take the bike home. Also, Ray Price H-D knows us, and they might try to have our bike repaired sooner than the dealerships in West Virginia.

After Craig departed, my driver and I checked the website of the truck rental to get walking directions and find out what time they open for business. The truck rental place was open on Sundays and they open at noon. It was about a three mile walk. My driver brought a bottle of water for me and we left the hotel late in the morning. On the way to the truck rental place, we walked by the car rental place. They were closed. My driver and I talked while we walked. We both preferred to rent a small moving truck rather than a car because that would mean we could get the bike to Ray Price sooner. My driver crossed his fingers for luck. I would have crossed my paws, but I was busy using them to walk. My driver let me stop and sniff stuff along the way, so I was enjoying the walk.

In the distance, we saw two rental trucks and the store. There were two trucks on the lot! Hopefully, one would be available for us. We walked across a field with tall grass. It was a short cut to the store. About half way through the field, my driver started saying "Oooooo. Ooooo. Ahhhhh! Ouch! Ouch! Ouch!" He was grabbing at his leg. He was dancing around and yelling "Ouch! Ouch! Ouch!" I looked at him and tilted my head left and right in curiosity. I thought he wanted to play so I crouched and was ready to pounce. He unbuckled his belt, unzipped his pants and pulled his pants down to his knees. He was slapping at a black thing that looked like it was attached to him. I think it was a spider! I walked over to him as he slapped the critter off his leg. I tried to sniff and find it in the grass but couldn't find it. My driver put his pants on, and we trotted across the rest of the field. The grass was so high that I couldn't see more than a foot or two in front of me. I just followed my driver because he was mashing down the grass in front of me. Sometimes, I leaped in the air to look over the grass and to see where we were heading.

We arrived at an electronics store that happened to rent trucks. We were in luck! The larger truck was available. It was much larger than what we needed, but we didn't care. It took about 30 minutes to do the paperwork for the truck rental. I stayed outside and snoozed on cool concrete in the shade. My driver came out of the building and told me it was time to roll. My ears perked up when he said "rooooooll" and we walked quickly to the truck. We stopped at a store and my driver bought some ratchet straps, which we would need for the bike. We called J&J towing. Although they were closed, someone would meet us there. Those folks are pawesome!

My driver positioned the truck on the downhill part of a dirt road. Three guys helped my driver push the bike uphill. My driver slowly rolled the bike down the road, onto the truck's loading ramp and into the truck. I supawvised my driver in securing the bike in the back of the truck. It was getting warm and a bit humid, and it took my driver about 45 minutes to ensure the bike would not fall in the truck.

After the bike was secured, we went into the truck's cab. The truck had air conditioning! We stopped at the New River Gorge Bridge to take a look. It was a long walk down lots of steps, but it felt longer going back up the steps.

We stopped at a rest area in Virginia to stretch our legs. The truck didn't have cruise control, and my driver thought the truck had something called a "speed governor". We stopped at the same gas station near "Mayberry" that we stopped on the previous day. My driver refueled the truck, moved the truck to the back of the parking area, opened up the rear door, fetched one of my canned MREs from the saddlebag and my travel bowl. It was supper time! While I ate, my driver walked to the fast food section of the gas station. By the time he returned to the truck with a burrito, I already finished my dinner. He gave me water to wash down my dinner, and walked me to a grassy area to relieve myself while he ate his burrito.

I slept a lot in the truck's cab. We arrived home after midnight. My driver was tired and his leg was swollen in the area that critter was making a meal of his leg. The next morning, I stayed home with my mom while my driver took my bike to Ray Price.

While my Harley-Davidson was in the shop, Craig visited a number of veterans' memorials and cemeteries while rolling through West Virginia, Kentucky, Tennessee, Arkansas, Oklahoma, Texas, New Mexico, Louisiana and Mississippi. We followed Craig on social media and we prayed frequently for his safety. Craig carried the Fallen Heroes roster with over 6,700 names. It's hard to describe the emotions when you see a name on a head stone or a memorial and you realize you are symbolically carrying that person with you on a journey to honor Fallen Heroes and to honor our military service members, past and present.

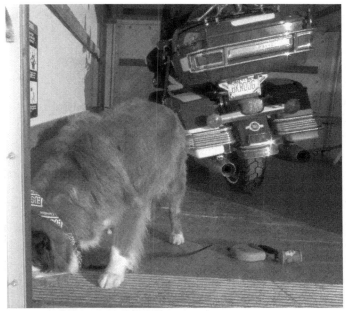

Supper time near Mayberry

Snoozing in the rental truck

My driver went back to work. His boss, Mark Burbank, had work for him to do until the bike was repaired. Mark left it open to my driver to resume his time-off if my bike was repaired quickly.

The problem with my Harley wasn't the gear pack. The rear pulley was chewed up and about a third of the drive belt teeth were sheared off. It appeared that maybe something got caught between the pulley and the belt. The Ray Price crew had my Harley-Davidson ready by Friday.

At about the time we were getting our bike out of the shop, Craig also had a problem with his bike. He took his bike to Thunderbird Harley-Davidson in Albuquerque, New Mexico with electrical problems. We had only one day built-in as a contingency, so when his Harley-Davidson was ready, he headed east.

My driver picked up my bike on Friday. We packed and loaded the bike on Friday night. On Saturday morning, we stopped at the Kipling Cross, then we rolled west to link-up with Craig. Craig was rolling eastbound, and my driver estimated we would likely linkup in Mississippi or Alabama.

We rode through Albemarle around mid-morning. My driver and I saw a display of military vehicles, so we stopped. It turns out that the man who owns the vehicles also owns the aviation museum in Charlotte. He allowed me to sit in his vehicles so hoomans can take pictures! We stayed there for over an hour and talked with some military men in uniform and with people who were interested in me.

We stopped at the Billy Graham Library in Charlotte, North Carolina. The gate guard questioned me, but I let my driver do the talking. He told us that I would not be allowed on the property, unless I had my service dog credentials. My driver explained our mission and that we just wanted a picture. The gate guard allowed us to enter the property and asked that I not dismount from the bike.

Sitting in one of the old military vehicles in Albemarle, NC

Visiting the Billy Graham Library

We stopped the bike under a shade tree near the library. A bus pulled in behind us and unloaded passengers. You can guess what happened when they saw me! My driver was concerned that the gate guard might be wondering why we were taking so long. I stayed in my saddle. After several minutes of sniffing many of the bus passengers, a security guard walked to us. He talked with us and took pictures of me. My driver assured him that we were there to just take some pictures and we would be on our way. He told us that we were not causing any harm and to take our time. It was great being among Christians!

We rode US-64 across North Carolina toward Chattanooga. By the time we reached Brevard, we rolled through scattered showers and fog. US-64 through western North Carolina was a beautiful ride with a lot of sweeps and curves.

We stopped at a waterfall that fell over part of a road. I think it's called Bridal Veil Falls. We intended to stop for only a few minutes – enough time to snap a few pictures. My driver parked near the waterfall. I thought he was going to ride through the waterfall and I became a bit nervous! He took pictures and I occasionally looked back at the waterfall to ensure it was not sneaking up on me. A few hoomans were there. They took many pictures of me. We intended to be at the waterfall for a few minutes, but we ended up being there about 30 minutes because of hoomans wanting pictures. My driver and I didn't mind. I enjoyed being petted while my driver talked about me, God and Jesus, and Fallen Heroes.

It was dark by the time we reached Chattanooga. It rained all night. I got hit with diarrhea and I had to wake my driver several times during the night. I like that my driver is in-tune with me and knows when I need to go outside. Fortunately, our hotel room was on the ground floor and the room door led directly outside. It was a short trot in the rain to a place where I could relieve myself. After my second trip in less than an hour, my driver gave me a pink tablet to help stop the diarrhea. It worked, because sometime during the night, I felt the urge, but nothing came out. My driver and I didn't get much sleep, and each time we went outside, we got wet in the rain.

The next day, we visited Chattanooga National Cemetery. It was drizzling as we rolled around the cemetery. We didn't know anyone interred at this cemetery. But, like every cemetery we visit, we were barkless to be riding on hallowed ground populated by the earthly remains of people who put others ahead of themselves. It was eerily quiet. I asked my driver if we were allowed to be on the property. We saw no visitors, no groundskeepers and no vehicles. Perhaps the rain kept people away. We spent about 30 minutes at the cemetery. My driver dismounted a few times. He tried to help me dismount, but I didn't want to get my paws wet.

At a Chattanooga hotel for the night before the rain

Visiting Chattanooga National Cemetery

When a man or woman joins the military, they are willing to sacrifice their lives for our freedoms. Although we didn't know anyone at the cemetery, I'm surprised that very few people go to a National or Veterans' cemetery – even if nothing more than a thank-you gesture.

We departed Chattanooga in rain. As we rolled through northwest Georgia into Alabama, the rain was heavier. We pulled into a truck stop and parked under an awning. My snout and goggles were wet, but the rest of me was still dry even though we had been in rain for over an hour.

We rolled through very heavy rain towards Birmingham. Sometimes, we were travelling as slow as 30 mph. Once we reached the north side of Birmingham, it was partly sunny and warm. My driver was wearing a rain suit, but he was soaked to the skin. That's how hard it was raining. Me? I was mostly dry. Part of my shirt was damp, but most of my shirt was dry. At a gas station, my driver stripped out of his rain suit. He tried to do a sexy strip dance in front of me. I just looked at him and yawned.

By the time we reached the hotel in the southern area of Birmingham, my driver's clothes were dry, except for the socks in his boots. We checked into the hotel, then rode south to visit the Alabama National Cemetery. It appeared to be a relatively new cemetery. It was quiet. We saw two visitors at a distance while we were there.

Later in the afternoon, Craig arrived at the hotel. Link-up successful! We rode to a well-visited area for dinner at a dog friendly restaurant. I had a hamburger – meat only. While Craig and my driver ate, I snoozed under the table.

The next day, we visited a memorial in Birmingham. It was very different than any memorial I visited. One area seemed like a large stone tomb. On the walls were the names of Fallen Heroes. There was an opening on one side of the structure in which the sun rays cast the image of a cross on the inner wall. It was pawesome! Craig and my driver read a few names of Fallen Heroes engraved on the wall from the Iraq and Afghanistan conflicts. They looked through their Fallen Heroes rosters to spot check to ensure they were in their books. Yup, they were! It's hard to explain the feeling of carrying a roster of names, then finding a specific name in your roster. I heard many hoomans say "Never Forget." Craig, my driver, and I are doing our part to remember their sacrifices.

Visiting Alabama National Cemetery

Following Craig Hardy through the pillars to the tomb-like structure

Inside the tomb-like structure with Craig Hardy

We rolled into the rest area on the Alabama/Georgia line. Our intent was a quick bladder break. But, whenever I roll into an area with lots of traffic and hoomans, we rarely stay a few minutes. I reckon a friendly dog on a motorcycle accompanied by friendly hoomans is an attraction.

At the rest area, I stayed with Craig while my driver went to the hooman potty building. When my driver returned, Craig went into the building. My driver and I were in the shade under a tree. My driver said a short prayer asking God for guidance on this mission. He asked for a sign that we were doing what He wants us to do. Less than a minute later, my driver and I heard a voice behind us ask "Have you ever heard of Freedom Biker Church?"

My driver turned around. It was Pastor Leon from Freedom Biker Church in Horn Lake, Mississippi. Wow! God answered swiftly!

I trotted to Pastor Leon and sniffed his shoes and bottom of his pants. Yup! I sniffed him before at a Freedom Biker Church service. He was going to Florida. How is it that a Pastor we know from Mississippi converge with a travelling biker dog and his crew at a rest area at that precise time? Coincidence? My driver and I believe that God orchestrated the link-up from the start. He knew my driver would need some form of assurance, particularly after the bike broke down.

We talked with Pastor Leon for a couple of minutes, and he had to go on his way. Soon afterwards, we were surrounded by several Buddhist Monks from Vietnam. One Monk spoke a little bit of English. They were interested in meeting me and taking pictures. I reckon a biker dog and his hoomans aren't something they see every day in Vietnam. My driver gave each of them one of my mission bracelets. I hope they don't get in trouble. My driver pointed out the Christian crosses on the bracelets. The Monk who spoke a little bit of English seemed to understand, and he said "OK".

After the Monks departed, we were surrounded by boys wearing red shirts. I'm unsure if they were brothers, or maybe a sports team with boys of different ages. I posed with them for pictures.

An hour later, Craig, my driver, and I were mounted on our bikes and rolling out of the rest area. Craig experienced what it's like to be me when we stop at a busy travel location.

In Atlanta, we visited the Marietta National Cemetery. This cemetery seemed to be older than most of the cemeteries I visited. The roads on this hilly cemetery were narrow and twisty.

We met-up with Craig's family in Atlanta. We waited for about an hour, but it was relaxing to be lying on shaded grass. After spending time with Craig's family, it was time to roll.

We arrived in Augusta soon after dark. Craig's dad had recently laid rocks on a steep uphill dirt road. Craig made it to the top with some effort. We got stuck halfway up, and Craig helped us by pushing. It was a steep path! It was dark, which didn't help.

Craig's mom had supper waiting for us. I ate my regular MRE dinner before my driver ate. Afterwards, they gave me some leftovers. Craig's mom put my driver and me in a bedroom. My driver slept on the floor with me. I think we both snored loudly.

The next morning, Craig's mom made a big breakfast. Craig and my driver reconnoitered the path downhill. While I was sniffing around, they found an alternate path to the bottom of the hill. We loaded the bikes, mounted up and rode the bikes to the bottom of the hill. At the gate at the bottom of the hill, we dismounted and said our "thank you's" and "see ya laters". On our way to the interstate, Craig pointed out the school that he attended and told us a story of the school over the CB radio.

In Columbia, we briefly visited the Fort Jackson National Cemetery. After leaving the cemetery, we decided to ride on US-1 north. In Rockingham, we stopped for lunch and soft serve ice cream! Mmmmmmmmmmm. I love ice cream, but it gives me smelly gas.

A few hours later, we were home. We spent two days at home before riding with Rolling Thunder NC1 to Washington, DC to attend Rolling Thunder over the Memorial Day weekend. It's amazing the number of hoomans we meet who refer to Rolling Thunder as a "parade". It's a demonstration or protest, not a "parade". The local news estimated 500,000 bikes staged at the Pentagon for the demonstration.

Rolling Thunder weekend was totally pawesome. Before we departed for our trip, Barbra Corbett talked with the owner of a hotel in Falls Church, Virginia to grant an exception to the no-pet policy so that I could stay with RTNC1 and RTNC2. We had a clean, comfortable room surrounded by bikers from many states. Before leaving my house, my driver wrote the addresses of several dog-friendly restaurants in Arlington. When my driver was a young Lieutenant in the Army, he was stationed in Arlington. He told me things changed a lot! Using the addresses, we were able to eat at "sit-down" restaurants instead of parking lots of fast-food places.

On Saturday morning, we rode with RTNC1 and visited Arlington National Cemetery, where we visited several Fallen Heroes, most of whom we attended their funeral or memorial service. Craig and my driver carried their Fallen Heroes rosters while they walked in Section 60. A few of the resting places we visited were of Bradley Beard, Lucas Elliott, Scott Brunkhorst, Ed Cantrell and his daughters, Isabella and Natalia, Samuel Griffith, Mark Adams, Ben Sebban, Orlando Gonzalez, Jonathan Grassbaugh, EJ Pate, and several more.

Eating beef brisket with my driver in Arlington

At the Ft Washington Harley-Davidson shop, we met Kristin, the Gold Star Wife of Carlos Santos-Silva, Sergeant First Class, US Army, Killed in Action 22 March 2010, Afghanistan. We told her about the Fallen Heroes roster onboard my Harley-Davidson. We pulled it out of the saddlebag and asked Kristin for her husband's name. When she saw the book, she couldn't speak, so she pointed to a patch with her husband's name. My driver asked her for his home state, and she replied Tennessee. My driver opened the Fallen Heroes Roster. It opened right to Tennessee and my driver immediately pointed to SFC Santos-Silva on the page. Coincidence? My driver and I know God was guiding us. With the thousands of names on hundreds of pages, what are the chances of the book opening to the exact page and my driver's eyes immediately going to the correct name? It also felt like God used us to brighten Kristin's day – to convey to her that there are people who care. Honor. Respect. Remembrance.

The day of the demonstration started at o'dark thirty. There were about 40 or so bikes with RTNC1 that departed the hotel for the Pentagon. I think another chapter linked-up so that we had one large group. It was a nice, cool ride to the Pentagon.

The Pentagon parking lot was a giant staging area. There were motorcycles as far as my eyes could see. We joined the RTNC1 members and walked to the other side of the parking lot. They were staffing a booth until it was time to roll.

Two members of Congresswoman Renee Ellmers' staff were guests of RTNC1. They spent time with the chapter at the Pentagon parking lot. The two staffers became bikers for the event and rode with two RT members.

I supawvised my driver in mounting a video camera on the back of my bike. He wanted to see how I respond to the crowds and to the number of bikes. During the demonstration ride, my driver identified Marine Corps Staff Sergeant Tim Chambers ("The Saluting Marine"). While in the saddle and rolling slowly, my driver returned the salute. The video camera caught the salute – it became one of our favorite clips.

My driver returning the salute of SSgt Tim Chambers, USMC – "The Saluting Marine"

At the end of the route, we parked in a field along with thousands of other bikes. We walked to the National Mall area between the Lincoln Memorial and the Reflecting Pool. We found a shaded spot with cool, green grass.

Congresswoman Ellmers' staff spent time with the group under the shade tree. I spent the time in the shade snoozing on the cool grass and meeting the hoomans around us between snoozes. Sometimes, my driver uses me as a pillow while we both snooze. Dale Chason snapped a picture, which became another of my favorites. That photo showed the connection between my driver and me. I love my driver.

After the event, RTNC1 invited us to join them for dinner. We went to a restaurant with outdoor seating. That was very considerate of them to go to a restaurant with outdoor seating. We were in the shade and the temperature was very comfortable, even for somedoggie with a fur coat! My driver ordered a hamburger for me. I ate quickly, so afterwards, I snoozed and occasionally woke up when I sniffed someone with food in their hand and headed my way. After returning to the hotel, I had my nightly MRE.

The next day, my driver and I rode home. We left early in the morning, ahead of RTNC1. The ride home was uneventful. There were lots of law enforcement officers on the interstate. I think we left early enough to avoid traffic back-ups on the interstate.

Before returning home, we stopped at the Veterans Memorial Park in Lillington, then to the Kipling Cross. We talk with God a lot. For us, the stop at the Kipling Cross is symbolic. It's a place that has a physical reminder that Jesus gave his life on the cross for us.

After Rolling Thunder, the USO contacted Ol' Bill (aka OB1 aka Jammer aka Our Smoke Chasin' Friend) to try to reach me and let me know about Operation Omaha. Being the USO Ambassadog, I joined the USO in welcoming a group of WWII veterans returning from a visit to the National D-Day Memorial in Bedford, Virginia. There were three buses. The Patriot Guard Riders escorted them to Dorton Arena at the Raleigh Fairgrounds. There were lots of hoomans in Dorton Arena, along with one furry guy: my biker dog furfriend Snoopy. After we returned home, we watched news video taken from a helicopter of the buses rolling through traffic with police escort and the Patriot Guard. That was pawesome!

The next day, we participated in a fund raiser for the Veterans Legacy Foundation. The first 20 or so who registered received one of my dog tags from Craig's cross-country mission. When we linked up in Birmingham with Craig during our modified cross-country mission, we decided that Craig should have all of the dog tags since he carried them almost across the USA. We also decided Craig should keep the US funeral flag. The VLF fund raiser was a pawruffic success. Congresswoman Ellmers was at our Fayetteville destination to welcome us! The restaurant provided us with a chicken tenders basket, fries, bottomless sodas, water and cookies. I shared part of one chicken tender with my driver, but I let him have the fries and root beer.

Chapter 31: Collapse

The remaining chapters are from Chewy's driver, Butch.

Chewy unexpectedly collapsed on June 26, 2015. I was on my way home from work. Jo called to tell me that Chewy was in the backyard under the deck. He did not seem to be doing well. When I arrived home, Chewy came to me from underneath the deck, but he seemed sluggish. He wasn't panting. I checked his gums and his tongue. Both appeared pink.

Chewy came inside and ate dinner. He followed his routine of going outdoors to relieve himself. He seemed to want to remain outside on the deck or in the breezeway.

Jo and I grabbed a quick fast-food dinner and returned home. I checked Chewy's gums again. It seemed to be getting pale. Jo and I contacted the Animal Emergency Clinic in Cary, North Carolina. We were advised that we could either continue monitoring Chewy, or bring him to the clinic. Jo and I decided to take Chewy on the 45-minute drive to the clinic. We arrived at about 2000 (8:00 pm).

The veterinarian examined Chewy and took x-rays. She was unsure Chewy would make it through the night. She told us that if we had not brought him to the clinic, he would not have made it much longer.

She was prepared to do surgery to remove a mass in his spleen, but she had to get him stabilized first. She prepared us for complications. Jo and I were trying to brace ourselves that Chewy would not likely survive surgery. Chewy was put on an IV and given pain medications.

Jo posted Chewy's condition on social media at about 2315 (11:15 pm). Debi Persinger read the post and asked Jo if she could post it on Chewy's page. Jo agreed. Around midnight, the vet suggested that Jo and I go home for a few hours.

Jo and I returned home and took quick showers. We wanted to be with Chewy, even if it meant sitting in a waiting area. While packing overnight bags, we received a phone call from the veterinarian. We returned to the clinic.

While we were away, Chewy was resting and the team worked to stabilize him. The vet noted other clinical signs that led her to believe that Chewy might also have adrenal cancer. At that point, she did not feel comfortable operating on Chewy, which is why she called us to return to the clinic.

The vet arranged for Chewy to be admitted to the North Carolina State University Veterinary Hospital and School. NCSU Vet Hospital is one of nine Level 1 Trauma Centers in the United States. Chewy seemed much better, but it was probably the pain medications helping him feel good. He was still not expected to survive the night, but he was comfortable.

There was heavy rain, thunder and lightning when I carried Chewy into the backseat of the truck at about 0130 (1:30 am). Jo, who does not like driving in the rain, drove to NCSU Vet Hospital while I sat in the backseat with Chewy. When we arrived at the hospital, I carried Chewy to the door, where waiting staff met us outdoors. Before entering the door, they took Chewy from my arms and carried him to the treatment area. Chewy was admitted to doggie ICU, where a team worked to stabilize him. The attending vet reviewed the x-rays and did an ultrasound. Their diagnosis was consistent with the vet at the Emergency Clinic.

While sitting the waiting area, Jo checked social media and saw hundreds of posts from people praying from around the world. Many were people we did not know, but they followed Chewy's adventures on social media. Jo and I were in tears, grateful for the loving prayers of many. Countless people around the world were united in prayer for a selfless, furry, little guy. Most of them probably never met Chewy. Jo read some of the social media posts to me. That's when I started realizing that Chewy touched people in ways I never imagined. Those posts from hundreds of people from around the world revealed to me that God was, in fact, touching people through one of His furry creatures that we call Chewy.

God answered those prayers for healing. Chewy made it through the night, but we saw he was uncomfortable. He perked up a little when they gave him pain killers, which was a bit comical to watch. I knew Chewy had to pee and was holding it. The vet allowed me to take him outside. He walked slowly and could not hold his leg up to pee, so he just stood on all four paws and let it pour.

The hospital had specific visiting hours. Family could not stay with the furkids. Jo and I left the hospital at about 0630 (6:30 am) to get some sleep while they continued working to stabilize him.

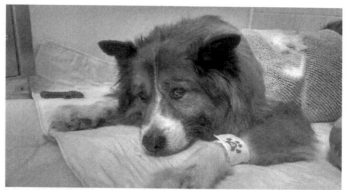

Visiting Chewy at NCSU Veterinary Hospital

I posted an update on Chewy's social media page a little after 0800 (8:00 am). A couple of hours later, Dr. Lindsay Warner called us. She works with Dr. Bailey at Animal Hospital of Peak Plaza. Doc Bailey was Chewy's primary care veterinarian since we adopted him. Doc Warner had cared for Chewy a few times since she joined the practice. Doc Bailey was out-of-town, but we trusted both docs. The staff learned about Chewy's condition on social media, which is what prompted the call from Doc Warner. Doc Warner provided us with her cell phone number and encouraged us to call her if we needed help with Chewy or had questions.

Jo and I returned to the hospital at 1530 (3:30 pm) to talk with the veterinarians. We are grateful that Doc Warner offered to help us. Our brains were on overload, so it was helpful talking with Doc Warner, who was not as emotionally attached to Chewy as Jo and me. Jo and I were on the path to making decisions for Chewy based on emotions. With God's help in guiding Doc Warner in providing recommendations, we believe Chewy had a chance to survive.

Jo and I grabbed a quick meal at about 1800 (6:00 pm), and returned to the Hospital for the 2030 (8:30 pm) visiting hour. Chewy wasn't feeling any pain, but he was out of it. He looked at Jo and me and would fight to stay awake. He would nod off, then wake up and just look at us while fighting to stay awake again. He would occasionally whimper softly, but I don't know if that was pain or the frustration of being drowsy and wanting to stay awake with us.

We brought him a Greenie. The vet said it was OK. A Greenie was one of his nightly treats. I know he couldn't read a clock (or could he?), but he always reminded us when it was time for his treat. He wasn't interested in taking the Greenie, which was an indicator to me that he was not feeling well.

He ate dinner a few hours before the visiting hour. It was a low fat soft food and it was equivalent to about 3/4 of a can.

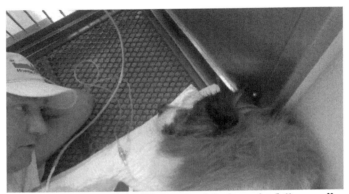

Spending time with Chewy in his hospital "room"

The vet told us that if Chewy is strong enough to be anesthetized or sedated for a CT, then that will probably happen on Monday. We were trying to gather as much information as possible before deciding on surgery. Doc Warner talked with us several times during the day. She also talked with Chewy's attending vet.

That evening, we were told by the vet that if Chewy is strong enough for surgery, they would consider operating. The surgeon is one of the best in the world. She explained that the surgery is one of the riskiest, so we have to take into consideration that he might not survive surgery. At that time, surgery appeared to be the path, but Jo and I continued praying for God to guide us and grant us the wisdom to make the decision that was best for Chewy. Chewy's social media page continued receiving countless posts of prayers.

During the afternoon visiting hour on Sunday, June 28, Allison Shackelford joined us in visiting Chewy. He seemed somewhat alert, so we took him outside. His heart rate and blood pressure were much better. The vet team did very well in getting him more stabilized. At that point, it looked like he would be OK to be anesthetized for a full body CT on Monday. At this point, Chewy had come a long way since Friday when we were told he might not make it through the night. The middle-of-the-night handoff from the Animal Emergency Clinic in Cary to the NCSU Vet Hospital was superb.

When we visited during the 2030 (8:30 pm) visiting hours, he was drowsy. He had a full round of meds at about 1900 (7:00 pm). He wasn't interested in any treats during our visit, but he ate dinner earlier in the evening and didn't vomit. Chewy and I lay together in his little room and he seemed comfortable knowing that Jo and I were with him. His heart rate and blood pressure were holding, so it continued looking good for him to be anesthetized for a full body CT scan.

Two days prior on Friday night, there were indicators of internal bleeding. The vet believes it encased his adrenal gland. On Sunday evening, the vet did not think that Chewy was still bleeding, but his platelet count was low, which was an indicator that his little body was fighting to stop the bleeding. One of the dangers emphasized to us is the clot popping off.

On Monday, Chewy was placed under anesthesia at 0900 (9:00 am) for a full body CT scan. Jo was with him during the morning visiting hour. She told me that Chewy appeared to be looking for me. I had to work, but I was able to leave at 1100 (11:00 am) to go to the hospital. We waited in the hospital until the next visiting hour at 1530 (3:30pm).

Chewy was released before the afternoon visiting hour. Before his release, we met with the veterinarian team. They were waiting for the surgical team to talk with radiology and make a recommendation. Jo and I were still unsure about surgery. Surgery was estimated to be $14,000, and ICU was estimated to be

$5,000. Our greatest concern was Chewy's quality of life. Jo and I agreed that if we proceeded with surgery, we would sell the bike and withdraw from our 401(k) funds.

When we arrived home, Chewy was groggy from the meds. He tried to stand, but he ended up dropping to the ground. I carried him from the truck to the house. He was home in familiar surroundings and scents.

Chewy liked to sleep on his ortho bed upstairs. I doubted he could walk up and down stairs, so I brought his ortho bed from upstairs. We placed it in his favorite snooze spot downstairs, which is the marble slab in front of the fireplace.

Resting at home

The medical team had explained what we needed to watch. We still had a difficult decision to make. We continued to appreciate the prayers for Chewy during that period. Our objective at that point was to make him comfortable and love on him. The vet said he might be able to take some short rides on the Harley-Davidson, but I was the best judge as to whether or not it would be OK for him. Regardless, his orders were rest.

Chewy didn't have an appetite. He was a bit smelly, and the vet told us before releasing Chewy that it was OK to give Chewy a bath. We have a large walk-in shower and a handheld sprayer we can attach. Chewy took a shower with me. He didn't like baths, but he always slept well afterwards. He dozed off while I was blow-drying him. He slept well during the night. In the morning, he moved to lay at the front door. Perhaps he thought he was resuming his role as the protector of the house, or perhaps it was because that is the best vantage point to see the living room, dining room, kitchen, and stairway.

Chewy came a long way since Friday when the vets weren't sure he would make it through the night. Prayers were answered and Chew-Chew had a little more time with us. I prayed that when Chewy's time came, God and Jesus would allow him to go quickly and painlessly to Heaven to be with the many Fallen Heroes and passing veterans who he honored alongside many Patriots and friends. That was a very hard time for Jo and me. Those who have or who will be experiencing the decision on their furchildren understand the emotions. We cried a lot.

During Chewy's first night home from the hospital, Jo and I prayed for Charlie and Dude, two doggie patients at the hospital.

On Tuesday, Jo bought some ground beef. We cooked Chewy a burger on a stove top grill so that the grease dripped out of the meat. Chewy ate the burger (about 6 ounces) and ate some cheese. He drank about 16 ounces of water. We were happy he ate and drank. He still wasn't able to stand up on his own, so I carried him outside frequently. He stood long enough to empty his bladder and took a couple of wobbly steps toward me so I could carry him back inside.

Jo also bought some Frosty Paws doggy ice cream. Chewy LOVES Frosty Paws. He nearly fell asleep a few times while licking the doggy ice cream. Did I state that Chewy LOVES Frosty Paws?

Normally, Chewy's breath is OK. Now, it was very smelly. He had a teeth cleaning only once in his life because his teeth have been in very good shape, probably from brushing, chew toys, and lots and lots of Greenies.

At about 1800 (6:00 pm) on Tuesday, Chewy's NCSU vet called. The surgery and radiology teams met. They believed there was an 80% probability that Chewy would not survive surgery. If he survived surgery, he probably would not survive recovery in ICU. If we did nothing, Chewy's estimated life was two to four weeks. Jo and I decided to not put Chewy's little body through surgery based on those estimates. Doc Warner had much to do with the vets becoming more open with us. So, we mentally prepared for Chewy's remaining weeks.

Chapter 32: Road to Improvement

All things considered, Chewy had a good day on Wednesday (July 1). He ate about five ounces of soft food for breakfast. He ate slowly, but he ate it all. He was a one-meal-a-day dog and always had dry food for snacking. Since he had internal bleeding and became anemic from the blood loss, I wanted him to eat to help build his strength. He seemed to understand.

I carried him outside in the morning and helped him stand while he emptied his bladder. I then carried him back to his ortho bed, then drove to the office.

Our grandchildren, Chase and Delanie, loved on him for most of the day. Around 1000 (10:00 am), Chewy got out of his bed and wobbled to the bedroom and looked around. Jo thought Chewy was looking for me. He plopped down near the front door. Jo and Delanie later helped him back to his bed.

I returned home during lunch to work the remainder of the day from home. My manager, Mark Burbank, was among the best managers for whom I had worked. For lunch, Chewy had a hamburger patty. He ate all of it slowly. Jo had to run an errand and she came home later in the afternoon with a rotisserie chicken for our dinner. Chewy's vet had told us that he could have broiled or baked chicken, but no skin. By the time Jo returned, Chewy seemed a lot perkier. Chewy ate about half of the chicken, and he let Jo and me share the rest of it. His normal routine is to go outside after dinner. He was slipping trying to stand up on the wood floor, so I carried him outside. He was wobbly, but I didn't have to help him stand when he pottied – the joys of little victories! He walked slowly back to the deck steps, but he stumbled and fell on the first step. I carried him back to his bed and pulled the rest of the chicken for him (about a small handful).

After watching the national news, I took a shower. Chewy wobbled to the bedroom and lay in front of the bathroom door to watch me – that was his normal routine. I was in tears from happiness that he was slowly returning to his routine. When I stepped out of the shower, Chewy wobbled to the front of the bed and lay down. Again, routine. Normally, after I'm dressed in pajamas, he lays in the hallway and diverts me to the laundry room, which is where his supper dish, water and treats are located. He didn't get there and plopped onto the floor. I followed the routine and brought him a Greenie from the room. He gave me a tail wag. The day ended well.

Doc Warner and the NCSU vet told us we could stop two of the meds since we were not going to put him through surgery, so the effects of those meds were wearing off.

On Thursday, Chewy had an appointment with Doc Warner to check his blood pressure, heart rate, and blood count. Clinical signs were good, but we did not know if he had hours, days or weeks. We had not thought beyond weeks.

Chewy's Harley-Davidson was in the shop to replace the rear tire. After his doctor appointment, he was with us to pick-up his bike. Chewy had to settle for riding in the backseat of the truck while I rode the bike home. Jo said he sat in the middle of the back seat, looked intently out the windshield to watch me on the bike, and occasionally whined. With about 100,000 miles in the saddle, Chewy was usually on the bike when the bike was on the road. Watching the bike while in the truck must have been odd to him. When we arrived at the house, I put Chewy in his saddle. I fired up the bike and we backed the bike into the garage. When we dismounted, he looked very happy and content, even if it was just a short "ride".

I did not have time to read the posts in Chewy's social media page. Jo stayed current and summarized them and named the posters. There is one post that she asked me to read. It was from Lori Featherston. In summary, she posted that with all the bad things going on the world, people were united for a dog and his driver. Jo and I continued to be amazed by the number of people who Chewy touched around the world.

Chewy's bladder seemed to fill more quickly as compared to before he collapsed. I slept lightly at night. Just as Chewy would detect my movement in the house, I quickly learned to listen for his toe nails on the wood floor heading toward the breezeway door in the kitchen. That was my signal to put on my slippers and go outside with Chewy. I carried him down the deck stairs, he urinated, then returned to the concrete pad at the base of the steps so I could carry him up the stairs. We did this three to ten times a night. He slept during the day while I was at work and Jo let him out a few times a day. Jo had a lower back fusion several years prior, and Chewy was too heavy for her to lift. Chewy could quickly move down the stairs, but climbing the stairs was difficult and his legs would sometimes give out and leave him straddled across steps.

Chewy had weekly appointments at Animal Hospital of Peak Plaza. The primary focus was managing his blood pressure and checking his platelet count. The concern was that if he had an internal clot, high blood pressure could blow the clot. If his platelet count remained low, his little body might not be able to stop a bleeder. His blood pressure remained good. Over the weeks, his platelet count returned to a better number. Chewy was mending.

Dr. Lindsay Warner and Chewy at Animal Hospital of Peak Plaza

Chewy quickly returned to his routine. Every Saturday morning, he and I made a four-egg cheese omelet. We returned to our Saturday morning routine of Chewy eating about one-fourth of the omelet, and he let me have the remainder.

After several months, Chewy began to appear stressed at night. He continued waking up several times at night to relieve himself, but he was able to trot down the deck stairs, and he learned to climb the stairs at an angle. At one of his appointments, we talked with Doc Warner about Chewy's behavior at night.

With Chewy's cataracts gradually worsening, she suggested leaving a light on. Perhaps Chewy was getting disoriented in the dark. That night, we left a living room lamp on. Chewy seemed much calmer at night from that point forward. For Chewy and his parents, Docs Bailey and Warner and their staff are fantastic!

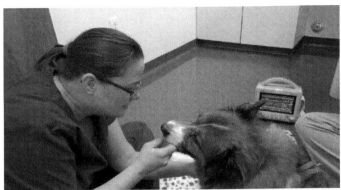

Tracy Vester, one of the caregivers at Animal Hospital of Peak Plaza who Chewy recognized

After a couple of months, we took a short ride on the bike. He eventually returned to riding, albeit short rides. We were selective on the events we attended. If the temperature and humidity combination were forecasted to be high, Chewy and I did not attend events. If an event required walking more than a few feet, we would not attend.

During spring and summer, Chewy and I frequently rode for 30-45 minutes after I returned from work. Our normal routine when I returned from work was to take a walk. The distance he could walk became shorter with each passing week. I believe that riding was an activity that he could still do and enjoy. More importantly, by me riding the Harley-Davidson only with Chewy, I believe Chewy felt that I was not abandoning him or leaving him behind. Each time we stepped into the garage, he would walk to the bike, sniff the bike in a few places, and look at me with wanting eyes – wanting to ride.

In December 2015, Chewy was filmed and interviewed for a segment of The Tar Heel Traveler, a television news story segment aired on Raleigh's WRAL. Chewy and I watched the Tar Heel

Traveler frequently for ideas about North Carolina destinations. Scott Mason's story about Chewy was very touching.

Taking a short ride in the neighborhood

In March 2016, a travelling USO film crew stopped in the Raleigh area to do a short video story about Chewy, the USO-NC's ambassadog. A few years prior, Chewy was featured in the first episode of a 10-episode television series about USO-NC. Jo and I were again touched at how a dog gained the interest of many people.

Chewy would ride about 2,000 miles over the next year. Compared to riding an average of 14,000 miles per year, this was a significant decrease in his saddle time, but he appeared to be happy to be with me in the wind.

Chewy continued to periodically attend Sunday service at Freedom Biker Church in Clayton or Fayetteville. He was welcomed because of his ministry. Yes, Chewy was a dog. Chewy is evidence that God can and will use anyone or anything to reach people – even a dog on a motorcycle and his driver.

Chewy had many friends at Freedom Biker Church. At the end of one service at Clayton sanctuary, Preacher Mike asked Chewy, Jo and me to come to the altar. Those in attendance (about 150+) joined us and encircled us. Christy Gonzales said a prayer for Chewy. I watched Chewy. He appeared to be looking at as many people he could see. His tail wagged slowly. He was surrounded by Christian friends. He seemed to understand that everyone was in a circle for him. I fought back the tears. I continued to be humbled and surprised that people would gather for a dog. I truly believe that God allowed Chewy to remain with us a few months longer because of the many prayers.

Spending time with family

Chapter 33: Passing to Heaven

Chewy passed peacefully at about 1245 (12:45 pm) on Monday, April 3, 2017. He was a member of our family for just over 13 years. He survived 22 months after collapsing and, at the time of his collapse, estimated to have two to four weeks. For the most part, he was not in pain. He seemed to have a few moments of discomfort, in which he would pass gas and appear to feel better.

The Bible was written for people. There is no mention in the Bible about pets going to Heaven. However, there is reference to lions and lambs laying side-by-side in Heaven. I read an article written by Billy Graham about pets in Heaven. Based on the reference of lions and lambs and Mr. Graham's article, I have hope that our pets are somehow serving God and they are waiting for us. Where many people have heroes who are athletes, actors, etc, my heroes are God and Jesus, and people like Billy Graham and Franklin Graham. Jo and I are grateful to God for the hope He gave us through His Son, Jesus, our Lord and Savior.

On the Saturday before he passed, Chewy seemed to be feeling well. He attended the funeral of a passing veteran, Robert Womble, in Lillington. It was a sunny and cool day. Chewy was among many friends of the Patriot Guard. While we stood on the flag line, Chewy chilled on the grass in the shade. I could tell by his demeanor that he was happy. A few people attending the funeral stopped to meet Chewy. A couple asked if Chewy wore a helmet and glasses, then stated they saw him riding – hopefully, not riding solo!

On the way to the funeral mission, we stopped in Kipling to check Chewy's post office box. He had a package from Tracy Stivers on behalf of the USO. When we returned home from the funeral mission in Lillington, we opened the package. I sat on the floor with Chewy to open the package and he was inserting his nose between my hands. The package contained a stuffed hedgehog toy, treats, and a note. He could smell the treats before the box was opened! He posed with the package contents for a photo.

On Sunday, Chewy attended a charity event in Fayetteville: Zuma 'Round Town with Doctah Steve. The ride is led by Steve Prescott, who raises funds for a number of non-profit organizations such as Autism Awareness, Special Olympics and more. There were about 100 bikes at the event. Most of the participants are veterans who knew Chewy, so he was among friends.

Up to this point, Bud Dunlap was writing stories for Behind Barz Motorcycle Magazine. In his stories was a character "Spirit Chewy", who helped people in Heaven. Chewy and Bud met for the first time at Zuma 'round Town. Jo and I are honored that Bud was using Chewy in his stories in a respectful way that seemed to be a reflection of Chewy's personality.

The ride started and ended at the same location, where two food trucks were serving lunch. Chewy and I shared some barbecue (no sauce). He met and sniffed more people, and greeted many friends he has known for many years. His biker dog friends and their drivers were there: Snoopy and his driver, Tim Wall, and Hercules and his driver, James Whitaker. After the event, Chewy and I mounted up to return home. The ride from Fayetteville to our home in Kipling is about 45-60 minutes, depending on the route. It was another beautiful day with cool temperatures and low humidity, so we took the long way home. When riding, I could not see Chewy behind me, but I could feel him when he snuggled against my back and placed his muzzle on my shoulder at the base of my neck. I know he was happy to be on the road with me.

On Sunday evening, Chewy and I went into the garage for something. I cannot recall the reason, but it was probably to plug the battery tender to the bike. I noticed Chewy sniffing a drop of oil under the back of the primary chain case cover. Over the years, when Chewy sniffed oil under the lawn tractor or the few times the bike had an oil leak, I praised Chewy. Chewy also took an interest whenever I worked on the bike. If I removed a part, I let him sniff it. Before I put a part on the bike, I let him sniff it. Chewy seemed to enjoy making me happy and receiving praise. He probably did not know the meaning of oil on the garage floor, but he understood he was doing something helpful. That evening was not any different. Chewy sniffed the drop of oil on the garage floor under the bikes primary case, then looked at me, sniffed the drop again, then looked at me. That was my cue to check it out. Yup. There was a drop of oil. I ran my fingers up the backside (interior side) of the primary cover and could feel oil as my fingers climbed. I speculated that the bearing seal was leaking. As with other times Chewy found oil, I praised him and petted him with an excited voice. Chewy went to sleep that night content that he did something very good – again!

On Monday morning, I commuted to work. Jo sent a text message to me during my commute, and I received it when I arrived at the office. Chewy collapsed. Jo contacted Animal Hospital of Peak Plaza and scheduled an appointment with Doc Warner for that afternoon. By 1030 (10:30 am), Jo called me and said she was taking Chewy to Doc Warner. I left the office and arrived at AHPP a few minutes after Jo.

When I saw Chewy, he was standing, but he looked like he didn't feel well. I looked at his gums and lips and they appeared pale. The clinical signs were not good. We had a choice of trying to stabilize him, or helping him to let go. Jo and I could see in Chewy's face that he was ready. We talked. At about 1215 (12:15 pm), we made the difficult decision to let his earthly body go to eternal sleep.

Doc Warner and Tracy prepared Chewy for the procedure. He was panting and his breath did not smell like it usually smelled. The last time his breathe smelled like it did was when he collapsed about 22 months earlier. Chewy and I took one last selfie before Doc Warner and Tracy returned to the room. Jo and I did not look at the pic.

Doc Warner explained the potential reactions, include loss of bowel and bladder control, as he passed. She injected something so that Chewy would feel no pain. When we were ready, Doc Warner injected the drug that would allow Chewy to leave his earthly body. Jo sat in a chair in front of Chewy. I was lying on the floor beside Chewy. There were lots of tears. I know veterinarians and vet technicians try to avoid becoming emotionally attached to their furry patients. Both were in tears, as were members of the AHPP team outside of the room. We could hear people sniffling. This dog named Chewy touched so many lives in his lifetime.

Chewy went to God and Jesus at about 1245 (12:45 pm). It was as if he quickly dozed off to sleep. No panting. No wimpering. No loss of bladder or bowel control. His passing was very peaceful. I felt that God and Jesus now had Chewy.

We tried several times to reach someone at the pet crematory. We left a message. Doc Warner and Tracy allowed us to move Chewy's body to the area with the labs and offices. We waited for the crematory to call. After about 30 minutes, Jo and I went to a sandwich shop next to AHPP. Although neither of us were hungry, we tried to eat. The crematory returned our call and we scheduled a time to take Chewy's body.

About 30 minutes before Chewy went to eternal sleep, I took a picture of him and me – our last photo together. Jo and I did not look at the photo until days later when I was second-guessing myself. That photo was helpful. Knowing Chewy, I could see in his face that he was ready. His eyes seemed to be telling me "It's OK, dad." I didn't realize it at the time, but I had my cheek on Chewy's forehead. When Chewy sensed I needed him, he put his cheek (muzzle) against my cheek. It was how Chewy and I comforted each other.

Days and weeks later, a number of people inquired about a memorial service or a memorial ride in honor of Chewy. A memorial service? For a dog? I never heard of a memorial service for a dog. Prior to a Sunday service in May, I talked with Floyd Baker, one of the pastors at Freedom Biker Church in Clayton. Floyd talked with Preacher Mike Beasley. A Celebration of Life was scheduled for June 24.

About 150 people attended Chewy's Celebration. We rolled Chewy's Harley-Davidson Electra Glide Ultra Classic into the church and placed his urn in his saddle. People rode to Clayton from as far away as Florida, South Carolina, Georgia and Tennessee. I was too distracted before the service that I did not setup a video camera. Paula Schronce, however, taped the service and posted the four-part video on social media.

Prior to the service, Floyd told me that if it feels like the Holy Spirit is taking over, to let it happen. If it does, I probably won't remember anything that I said. He was right.

The service started. Preacher Mike led us in prayer. Jim and Christi Kazakavage presented a picture plaque. I stood at the podium and looked at my typewritten notes. The words seemed jumbled and my brain did not seem to interpret the words. My presentation slides were all pictures, intended to serve as cues. I do not remember what I said. I remember hearing laughter when talking about Chewy. It was a blur.

Jo and I are very grateful to Paula for posting the videos of the service. When I watched the videos, I realized why people were laughing. I was telling them about Chewy's adoption, earning his name, his first ride, rides across the USA, the slobber factor, etc. I saw in the video that I put on my reading glasses to look at my typewritten notes, but I know the words were not being interpreted by my brain. I was talking about Chewy's adventures that we experienced together – I was completely off my "script". Most of the stories were already documented in the draft manuscript that eventually became this book. Chewy and I started writing his "pawtobiography" many years prior to his collapse. With the Holy Spirit guiding me, I didn't need notes because He blessed me with living the adventures with Chewy.

In August 2017, Betsy at Ray Price Harley-Davidson asked me for a picture of Chewy on his Harley and wearing a USO bandana. RPHD wanted to put Chewy's picture on the Patriot Ride shirt, which is an event that helps kick-off the Ray Price Capital City BikeFest in downtown Raleigh on the last weekend of each September. Most of the photos I have of Chewy were taken while riding. I sent several photos to Besty.

A few weeks later, Betsy sent me a picture of the tee shirt. I was at work and in tears. I posted the picture on Chewy's social media page. Shortly afterwards, RPHD received requests from people to purchase the shirt. The shirts were intended for the participants of the Patriot Ride. Proceeds of the Patriot Ride go to USO-NC and the US Veterans Corps. With the number of requests being received, RPHD allocated shirts to be sold through their website. Proceeds from the sale of those shirts would also go to USO-NC and USVC. Within hours, the shirts were sold out! RPHD ordered another batch of shirts and ensured there were enough shirts for the Patriot Ride participants. A few days before the event, the sale of shirts available through RPHD's online store was discontinued so there would be shirts available at the event. Shirts were shipped across the USA. Jo and I were humbled by the number of people purchasing shirts and helping one of the organizations that Chewy represented: the USO of North Carolina.

The last photo of Chewy and his driver together – about 30 minutes before Chewy went to eternal sleep

Chapter 34: Chewy's Missions and Events

The best I can determine, the following is a list of missions and events in which Chewy participated. I'm sure this is not all inclusive, but it is the best list I can build based on information that Chewy and I had. As you can see, Chewy did a lot during his short years with us. Some told me that Chewy did more in his short life than many people do throughout their entire human life with regards to helping people and non-profit organizations. Perhaps he didn't attend as many military funerals and memorial services as many Patriot Guard Riders, but he certainly attended more than the majority of Americans. Please, never forget those who gave their lives while in service to our country.

In each list, the date at the end of each record is the date of the funeral, memorial service, or event.

The following are the Patriot Guard missions, military funerals and memorial services that Chewy attended of those who gave their lives while in service to our country.

2008
- Shawn Simmons, Master Sergeant, United States Army, 5 Jul 2008

2010
- Ross S. Carver, Lance Corporal, United States Marine Corps, 9 Sep 2010
- James F. McClamrock, Private First Class, United States Army, 17 Sep 2010 & 3 Oct 2010
- Nathan Dutmer, Major, United States Army, 30 Nov 2010
- Willie A. McLawhorn Jr., Sergeant, United States Army, 18 Dec 2010

2011
- Amy Renee Sinkler, Private First Class, United States Army, 27 & 29 Jan 2011

- Curtis "KiKi" Yannone, Sergeant, United States Army, 4 Feb 2011
- Jared Kelley, Specialist, United States Army, 23 & 25 Mar 2011
- Jamal Bowers, Master Seargeant, United States Army, 25 Mar 2011
- James H. Graff, Captain, United States Air Force (remains identified and returned from Vietnam), 10 Jun 2011
- Aaron Blasjo, Sergeant, United States Army, 10 Jun 2011
- Jeffrey Sherer, Sergeant, United States Army, 14 Jun 2011
- Mark Bradley, Sergeant, United States Marine Corps, 24-25 Jun 2011
- Ralph Pate, Gunnery Sergeant, United States Marine Corps, 6 Jul 2011
- Lucas Elliott, Specialist, United States Army, 23 Jul 2011
- PJ Levy, Lance Corporal, United States Marine Corps, 17 & 20 Dec 2011

2012

- Edward Cantrell, Chief Warrant Officer 2, United States Army, 14-16 Mar 2012
- Trevor Adkins, Specialist, United States Army, 20 Jul 2012
- Donna R. Johnson, Staff Sergeant, United States Army, USA, 13 Oct 2012

2015

- Nicholas McGehee, Staff Sergeant, United States Army, 10 Jan 2015
- Matthew Wilkinson, Staff Sergeant,United States Army, 30 Oct 2015
- Donald Stewart, Staff Sergeant, United States Air Force, remains identified and returned from Vietnam, 9 & 11 Nov 2015

2016

- De'Von Maurice Faulkner, Aviation Mate, United States Navy, 1 Oct 2016

The following are the Flags for Fallen Military ceremonies that Chewy attended to honor those who gave their lives while in service to our country.

2011
- Michael Rodriguez, Specialist, United States Army, 25 Sep 2011

2012
- Calvin Harrison, Sergeant First Class, United States Army, 29 Jan 2012
- Gifford Hurt Jr, Private First Class, United States Army, 11 Mar 2012
- Scott Badgley, Master Sergeant, United States Marine Corps, 18 Mar 2012
- Jeffrey Webb, Lance Corporate, United States Marine Corps, 3 Jun 2012
- Steven Jewell, Specialist, United States Army, 7 Jul 2012

2013
- Christopher Henderson, Sergeant First Class, United States Army, 15 Sep 2013

2014
- Adam Ginett, Technical Sergeant, United States Air Force, 28 Sep 2014
- Austin Monk, Specialist, United States Army, 5 Oct 2014

2015
- James F. McClamrock, Private First Class, United States Army, 30 Oct 2015

The following are funerals and memorial services that Chewy attended for passing veterans. A few veterans had no family members to claim their remains. In those cases, the Patriot Guard

Riders became their family that day, held a service to honor their service, and interred their earthly remains.

2010

- Scott Farley, 7 Jun 2010
- Donald Berndt, 1LT, USA, 6 Jul 2010
- Harvey Mann, 13 Jul 2010
- James Chaney, 10 Dec 2010

2011

- Angel de la Cruz, 7 Jan 2011
- Ben Perry, 23 Jan 2011
- Donald Rumppe, 17 Feb 2011
- Lyle Davenport (a friend), 18 Feb 2011
- Clyde Barker, 9 Mar 2011
- Frank Buckles (that last American WWI veteran), 15 Mar 2011
- John Warren, 3 Apr 2011
- Mark Wilson (family friend), 23 Apr 2011
- Darleen Zupo, 25 Apr 2011
- William McLawhon, 3 Jun 2011
- Jerry Gober, 29 Dec 2011

2012

- Robert McCollum, 7 Jan 2012
- Ed Williams (friend), 2 Apr 2012
- Mark & Suzette Jones, 25 Jun 2012

2014

- Rudy Hendrix (friend), 8-9 Mar 2014

2015

- Rodney Parker (friend), 4 Mar 2015
- Lawrence Wilson, Jr., 7 Mar 2015

2016

- Bettie Rolf, 31 Jan 2016

- Craig Hutchinson (friend), 6 Feb 2016
- Steve Benjamin, 15 May 2016

2017

- Robert Womble, 1 Apr 2017   (Chewy's last mission)

Chewy participated in a few missions to help Wounded Warriors.

2010

- Cory Remsburg, Staff Sergeant, United States Army, 30 Jul 2010
- Escorting Wounded Warriors to Patriot Hunts, 4 Dec 2010

2012

- Tyler Jeffries, Specialist, United States Army, 22 Dec 2012

2013

- JB Kerns, Corporal, United States Marine Corps, 11 May 2013

The following are military-related events in which Chewy participated.

2009

- Patriot Run supporting Fisher House, 4 Apr 2009
- USO Freedom Ride, 15 Aug 2009
- Rolling Thunder NC4 POW Honor Ride, 6 Sep 2009

2010

- Lost Heroes Art Quilt, 13 & 21 Mar 2010
- CVMA NC 15-1 Charlie Mike honoring Vietnam War POW/MIA, 6-7 Aug 2010
- Rolling Thunder NC4 POW Honor Ride, 22 Aug 2010
- USO Freedom Ride, 11 Sep 2010
- Blue to Gold Ceremony, 23 Oct 2010
- Wreaths Across America, 11 Dec 2010

2011

- XVIII Airborne Corps deployment, 15 & 22 Jan 2011
- Gold Star Mothers meeting, Dogwood Chapter, 22 Jan 2011
- Blue to Gold Ceremony, 19 Mar 2011
- The Wall That Heals, 29 Mar 2011
- Month of the Military Child, Ft Bragg, NC, 4 Apr 2011
- Triangle Flight of Honor, 19 Apr 2011
- Warriors on Water, 29 Apr 2011
- Rolling Thunder NC4 POW Honor Ride, 18 Jun 2011
- CVMA NC 15-1 Charlie Mike honoring Korean War veterans, 5-6 Aug 2011
- USO Freedom Ride, 10 Sep 2011
- Operation Helping Hands for Heroes at Benson Mule Days, 24 Sep 2011
- Ride for Patriot Rovers, 1 Oct 2011
- Patriot Rovers awareness, 16 Oct 2011
- Triangle Flight of Honor, 26 Oct 2011

2012

- Gold Star Mothers meeting, Magnolia Chapter, 25 Feb 2012
- Visit to USO Ft Bragg, 15 Mar 2012
- Escort Vietnam Veterans Memorial to Charlotte Motor Speedway, 29 Mar 2012
- Vietnam Veterans Homecoming, Charlotte, NC, 31 Mar 2012
- Triangle Flight of Honor, 18 Apr 2012
- Rolling Thunder NC4 POW Honor Ride, 16 Jun 2012
- Gold Star Children at Camp Rockfish, NC, 24 Jun 2012
- USO Scoops for Troops, 21 Jul 2012
- CVMA NC 15-1 Charlie Mike III honoring World War II veterans, 3-4 Aug 2012
- Veterans Day parade as guest of CVMA NC 15-1, Fayetteville, NC, 10 Nov 2012

2013

- Month of the Military Child, Ft Bragg, NC, 8 Apr 2013
- USO Scoops for Troops, 20 Jul 2013
- Veterans Legacy Foundation, 5 Oct 2013
- USO Freedom Gala, 19 Oct 2013

2014

- Operation Omaha, Dorton Arena, Raleigh, NC, 6 Jun 2014
- War on Terror Memorial, 14 Jun 2014
- Visit to USO Jacksonville, 2 Aug 2014
- USO Freedom Ride, 6 Sep 2014
- Veterans Day Ceremony, Wake Forest, NC, 9 Nov 2014

2015

- Vietnam Veterans Welcome Home, Goldsboro, NC, 28 Mar 2015
- Month of the Military Child, Ft Bragg, NC, 13 Apr 2015
- Wreaths Across America, 12 Dec 2015

2016

- Gold Star NC Highway 24 Dedication, 6 Aug 2016
- War on Terror Remembrance, 11 Sep 2016
- Wreaths Across America, 17 Dec 2016

As one can see, Chewy did a lot in his life.

Tongue in the Wind

Chapter 35: GOD, Not "Coincidence"

At Chewy's Celebration of Life, USO volunteers setup a refreshment table. Some of the Gold Star Mothers volunteered with the USO and were in attendance. Many years ago, Chewy met Tammy Eakes, the Gold Star Mother of Lance Eakes, Sergeant, US Army, killed in action 18 April 2008, Operation Iraqi Freedom. After the service, Tammy realized a connection to Chewy and talked with me. Chewy's first ride occurred on the same day that Lance gave the ultimate sacrifice for his country. Chewy and I were with Tammy at a number of events over the years. Chewy knew Tammy, as he did a number of Gold Star Mothers. We knew of Lance, but his funeral occurred before Chewy's first Patriot Guard mission.

Chewy's life was full of "coincidences", but there were too many to be random events. What are the chances that Chewy would select two names who we did not know at a memorial in Irvine, California? Then, days later, we met a Marine's high school coach in Albuquerque, New Mexico. Weeks later, we met another Marine's parent in Garner, North Carolina, that Marine's sister through USO-NC and that Marine's brother who built the War on Terror Memorial in Holly Springs, North Carolina. Likewise, what are the chances that a North Carolina soldier would give the ultimate sacrifice on the same day that Chewy took his first ride on April 18, 2008 – and he later met that soldier's mother?

Chewy could not speak in human terms that we could understand. But, over the years, Chewy touched a number of hearts and was accepted by Gold Star Mothers for what he portrayed: honor, respect and remembrance. After Chewy's earthly body went to eternal sleep, we learned of the connection between Chewy and Lance Eakes. Coincidence? No. God used Chewy. I witnessed how He used a furry dog – a dog who seemed to be discarded and facing death as a young animal. Chewy was indeed blessed by God. Much of what I learned after Chewy went to be with God and Jesus were reminders that people around the world followed Chewy's adventures on social media – Chewy's life had meaning far beyond what I could have ever imagined.

I heard some people refer to Chewy as a "legend". Chewy was not a legend. People saw a dog and his broken dad trying to serve God using the tools and resources He provided. God gives each of us tools and resources to serve Him and to reach people. The resource could be a dog, a motorcycle, a boat, a fishing rod-and-reel, a friendship, or people you never met.

Was it a coincidence that I met Dr. Baity at the Airborne Special Operations Museum? Was it a coincidence that Dr. Baity told me that my purpose was to cast seeds of salvation? Or, was it all part of God's plan for Chewy? Our pastor at the time made it clear that a dog and a motorcycle do not make a ministry. Yet, prior to that conversation, he explained in his sermon how a bass boat and rod-and-reel are tools for a ministry. After my brief encounter with Dr. Baity, it became clear to me that God allowed me to build my riding skills for over 40 years. He gave me the ability to connect with dogs. He put Chewy in my life. He gave me decent writing skills. He gave me skills to build Chewy's website. He opened the doors for me to write articles about Chewy's adventures. He put Behind Barz Motorcycle Magazine in our path. Coincidences?

In October 2017, Freedom Biker Church in Clayton placed Chewy's photo on the trophy wall – a wall containing pictures of Freedom's Christian bikers who were called to Heaven. I questioned a dog being on the wall. I held back tears when Floyd Baker told me that it was discussed and Chewy represented a ministry to plant seeds with people on the road. The mission of Freedom Biker Church is to reach unchurched bikers. Chewy certainly did that. Chewy reached people around the world through his website and social media.

I believe God used Chewy to teach me lessons. Lessons on unconditional love, trust, judging, honor and respect. I never hit or beat Chewy. I admit giving him a pop on the backside to get his attention, and most of the time Chewy thought I wanted to play. God gave me pops during my life to get my attention, too.

It didn't matter what I was going through. Chewy was always there for me. Chewy's love was unconditional, just as I'm certain all dogs show unconditional love to their people. Chewy just wanted to be with me and go where I go. God's and Jesus' love for each of us is unconditional. They want to be with us. They are with us where ever we go. The only way to go to Heaven is by accepting Jesus, God's Son, as your Lord and Savior. I did. Although it hurts that Chewy is no longer with me, I know I will see him again.

When I adopted Chewy, he was fearful of people. He showed signs of being physically abused when he was put in the kill shelter. Chewy would run if he saw a person with an object in hand. The first time Chewy saw me with a broom in my hand, he ran from me in the house. When I tried to calm him, he urinated in submission. I was going to use the broom to sweep the sidewalk.

I worked to gain Chewy's trust. As a biker dog, Chewy learned to trust people. He eventually became the dog that many people loved to see and looked forward to meeting at events. He learned that all bikers are good and trustworthy. Regardless of a person's history, Chewy never judged anyone. Chewy taught me not to judge people, but, I'm human. Trying to avoid being judgmental is difficult, particularly if I'm hurt by someone or someone is disrespectful. In those cases, I looked at Chewy and prayed that God would give me the traits that Chewy displayed.

I thought I conveyed honor and respect, but Chewy taught me aspects of honor and respect that I had not previously displayed. Sometimes, honor and respect is displayed by not saying anything. Thousands of men and women will attend a military funeral and stand quietly with a flag. They expect nothing in return. Chewy and I stood quietly on many flag lines. While a small handful seemed to want attention and recognition, they received their reward, which was the attention of others. But, for those silent people standing in honor and respect, your reward awaits you from our Father, if you accept His Son as your Savior.

Being with a biker dog tends to draw attention. Through Chewy, I learned that I can take photos and videos at funerals, and create memorial videos to honor our Fallen in a respectful approach. Initially, those videos encountered resistance, particularly from the small handful of judging people seeking personal attention and recognition. God put Chewy in the hearts of many Gold Star Mothers who defended our actions as being honorable and respectful to their sons and daughters. In turn, that led organization leaders to understand that honor and respect can come in many forms. God used people to clear the way for Chewy and me to create dozens of videos in honor and remembrance of Fallen Heroes and Passing Veterans.

If you are the parent of a furchild, what did your furchild teach you? Is it possible that God is using your furchild? I know God used Chewy to teach me.

I know I'm not perfect in the eyes of people. But, I feel that in Chewy's eyes, I was perfect to Chewy. As a child of God and a Christian, I know God forgives me for my imperfections. I miss Chewy. With what I was going through before Chewy entered my life, I believe God put Chewy in my life to keep me on the path to eternal salvation through Christ. As long as I stay on the Christian path, I know I will spend eternity with God, Jesus, my wife, my family who accept Jesus as their Savior, Chewy, my other furkids, and my friends who accept Jesus as their Savior.

You control where you will spend eternity. Will I see you when I'm with God, His Son, Jo, my family, and the furry guy God gave me on Earth?

In January 2018, Jo noticed a puppy at an adoption event. That puppy's face looked a bit like Chewy. At the time, we weren't looking to adopt. We adopted him. In honor of Chewy, his name is Charlie – short for "Charlie Mike" – "Continue the Mission".

Lord, Jo and I thank you for putting Chewy in our lives and blessing us through him. Jo and I witnessed so many of Your blessings that occurred through Chewy that there are too many to simply be coincidences. Jo and I know in our hearts that You are with us and You used Chewy to reach people. I do not fully understand Your reasons, but we pray that we did it right in Your eyes. Thank You for allowing us to serve You. In Your precious and Holy Son we thankfully pray, AMEN.

Chewy was Jo's and my furchild. He was my therapy dog ... a biker dog ... a friend to many ... a furry representation of trust, faith, honor and respect. Chewy was a gift from GOD.

Tongue in the Wind

21016852R00144

Made in the USA
Middletown, DE
12 December 2018